Praise for Nudge

"In her book, *Nudges from Your Spirit,* Melissa shares stories of transition from a place of fear and uncertainty into one of trust. Learning to listen and connect to the spirit within is a subject I have spent many years teaching to my students, and Melissa has embraced those teachings and deepened her own connection to spirit. Some resonate with the angels; for others, spirit speaks to them while they practice yoga; and for Melissa, it has been the moon and the elements, and spending time in nature. This book can help you discover your own connection and how to strengthen and trust in the spirit within and around you."

~**Sunny Dawn Johnston**, Bestselling Author of
Invoking the Archangels and
The Love Never Ends

"Melissa Corter is a new breed of Shamanism tossed in with a beautiful psychic/medium added to a huge and open heart that supports this earth and everything living thing on it to draw closer to its most divine self. Her language and writing will hit you right in the heart where it belongs!"

~**Jodie Harvala**, Creator of *The Spirit School*,
Author of *The Magic of Space Clearing*
and *The ABC's of Intuition*

"*Nudges From Your Spirit* is a must-have for anyone who wants to learn how to use their intuition to create a better life. Melissa lays out a fabulous step-by-step plan that is easy to use and works! I highly recommend this book (and process) to everyone!"

~ **Flora Sage,** Six-time Author,
Mentor, Spiritual Empowerment Coach
& Intuition Expert

"In *Nudges from Your Spirit,* the gifted Melissa Corter has outdone herself with this gem! This book not only deepens your connection to spirit, but urges you to delve deep within and develop your own gifts and intuition through exercises and journaling prompts weaved throughout its pages. No matter which page you open to, there seems to be an insightful message waiting that's Divinely designed just for you and what you're experiencing at the time. The energy she's put into creating this book is felt on every single page. A beautiful masterpiece by a wise and gentle soul."

~**Shanda Trofe,** Bestselling Author of *Authorpreneur*
and *Write from the Heart*

NUDGES FROM YOUR

SPIRIT

Melissa Corter

NUDGES FROM YOUR SPIRIT

By Melissa Corter

Published by

Transcendent Publishing
P.O. Box 66202
St. Pete Beach, FL 33715
www.transcendentpublishing.com

First Edition December 2016
Second Edition November 2017

ISBN-10: 0997520965
ISBN-13: 9780997520965

Printed in the United States of America.

Acknowledgment & Dedication

To my "soul tribe": Thank you for being patient with me as I learned how to listen to you ... and furthermore, to take action.

This book is dedicated to my son Jared: May you always remember how much love, support, and guidance there is for you, seen and unseen. I hope your discovery of the spirit world unfolds as beautifully as mine has. I love you.

Contents

How to Use This Book

This book is designed to help you discover your spiritual strengths, and then how to home in on them, deepening your connection to spirit. There is no right way or wrong way to do this, but having said that, you may benefit by breezing through the book once to get a feel for what you are drawn to discover. Taking the time to do the provided exercises will enhance your connection to spirit, and you will grow and expand if you commit to doing the soul-work. Listen to your guidance to determine what is right for you, for if you do this, you will understand the true intention of this book.

Listening to your inner spirit will always guide you unerringly, without equivocation, and in every circumstance. This journey of life is a process, an unfolding of events that are meant for our highest good. The more frequently you can connect with this idea, the easier it becomes to find the gifts and lessons in our past experiences, moving us into a place of learning to witness them in our current experiences as they appear. Trust in yourself and allow your spirit to open to the flow of this guidance. I am excited to share this journey with you.

YOU DO NOT HAVE To Settle

Introduction

Learning to listen to my spirit has been a long and tumultuous journey, continuing to unfold as I wander farther along my path and deepen my spiritual connection. Nudges from your spirit come about by necessity. I believe in my heart that my life would be vastly different had I not learned how to listen to my spirit. Large chunks of my life were painful and traumatic, yet there is no space for a single moment of regret in my being; my path has been difficult, but I would not change a thing. My path + my challenges = my possibilities + my progress.

When writing this book, a theme began to formulate beneath the surface of all sections, reinforcing my belief that if we open our eyes and shift our perspectives on struggle and fear, a magnificent awareness will arise. There is an opportunity to become a witness to our past, detach from trapped emotions, and free up energy to powerfully create life in the present moment. Over and over, I will reiterate the importance of the present moment to ease the process of connecting with your spirit and listening to your guidance. Understanding the vast potential we all hold within allows your spirit to open up doorways that you may never have known existed. I cannot promise you it will be an easy ride, but I can promise you there is a greater part of you that doesn't want it to be easy anyway ... everything is happening FOR you, not to you.

We need contrast in life; this is one of the gifts that my passion for photography revealed to me early on. Without contrast we would float through life missing out on many magnificent gifts and lessons, neglecting to discover the potential of who we are at the core. It is in the days and nights when we question our soul's purpose, "Why do we exist?", and "What we are here for?", that the inquiry reveals an answer. It would not be possible for you to have a question if the answer did not already exist. The question does not arise within you from your pain, the question arises because your spirit is calling you to expand and step forward, release your fear and allow yourself to be seen. This may feel challenging to wrap your heart around, when the old stories and patterns of self-sabotage begin to arise. Not to worry, each and every one of us encounters some old programming and you can learn how to discover it before it dictates your next actions.

As we journey through this book together, keep in mind that I understand the difficulties and challenges we face with connecting and listening to spirit, especially when you may be surrounded by people, situations, or experiences that are showing you something different from what you're feeling inside. I grew up in a household that exemplified this in my daily experience, and in my body, mainly my solar plexus area, I could feel things were often not quite right, yet my outer world reflected back to me conversations and actions that made me dismiss what I was feeling.

Imagine your best friend just had a fight with her boyfriend. She has tears filling her eyes, and you witnessed the fight happen directly in front of you. You ask if she is ok, and with tears still coursing down her cheeks, she smiles and says, "Of course, why wouldn't I be?" She acts like the argument never happened and tries to convince you that you are mistaken and did not see what you know that you saw. In your mind, you are certain of what you just witnessed and yet her words and responses are not making sense. Some of us have had these experiences because we witnessed another aspect of the situation, in which we dismissed what the person said and instead trusted our own eyes. What if the same experience occurred and you did not witness it but saw your friend moments after the argument? All of a sudden your stomach or chest warns you something is not right, then you ask if she is ok, but she gives the same response, "Of course, why wouldn't I be?" This time you dismiss your feelings because you have no evidence and your friend has only given you feedback indicating you must be mistaken. We have this experience all the time, and discount our own guidance because we do not have immediate evidence. My intention is to help you recognize that you are picking up on energy all of the time; just not necessarily trusting in what you feel, think, or know, because the feedback isn't quite solid or clear.

This experience is common for individuals who have grown up in a household with alcoholics, drug addicts, substance abuse of any kind, or even various mental illnesses. In my particular situation, family members loved me and truly thought they were doing the best they could to shield and protect me. So they never argued in front of me, and they tried to hide their discomfort and unhappiness, yet the suppression of these emotions was palpable in the room for me. As a sensitive child, I could feel all the unspoken emotion and learned how to stuff these unhappy feelings in my body from a very young age. When this process would occur, subconsciously I believed my feelings were wrong, because there was no validation at that time. I believed for many years that there was something wrong with me and I learned very quickly to not trust in myself or my intuition. My intuition along with spirit was trying to guide me to see and feel the energy in the room, which in turn manifested as an unsettled heaviness. I could feel the sadness, the pain, the sorrow, and these feelings and emotions would linger until I sought to clear them.

As a child, not knowing any better, I did what came natural;

wanting to please people and feel good, I acted like a sponge or a vacuum cleaner, sucking up everybody's pain in order to lessen it, while ignoring my own. In my innocence and naivety, I discharged the emotions in the ways over which I had control, such as crying; so often that I was known as the crying child. The other way I learned to dismiss my feelings was to avoid them altogether and tamp them down with distractions such as food, TV, and sometimes creative outlets like music and photography.

In my household, food was always an issue between myself and my siblings. Whether it was the lack of food, or an abundance of the wrong foods, a harmonious balance did not exist. Somewhere in my innocence I discovered that I could self-soothe. Eating the wrong foods or even too much of anything became a pattern. This evolved into smoking, then moved into other destructive behaviors such as drinking, drugs, unhealthy relationships, and excess of any kind. I share this with you not to point out what was wrong, because I do not regret what has happened in my life; it is to help you recognize the possibility that you may have learned to adapt, dismiss, or suppress in your own world those difficulties you encounter by whatever means that might be for you.

I hope this book brings you peace while also opening you up to the guidance that is always available to you in every moment, every experience, and every situation. Some will take a different path; some will receive illumination in different ways. There is no right or wrong way to follow your spirit, all that matters is that you start the process and learn to nurture and develop it through the truths and lessons you receive. I will help you discover that there are numerous avenues by which to receive information and to strengthen your various gifts. We are never alone, and every moment is a new opportunity for us to expand and grow; we forget that we do not need to do this alone. As you read through this book, trust what you feel, recognizing that my ideas for doing anything, including my personal beliefs, philosophy, and techniques, may not be your way. I believe in following what resonates with you, and leaving the rest behind. I simply offer you tools and insights to always trust your own guidance and allow your own inner spirit to reveal what works for you.

We have stopped for a moment to encounter each other, to meet, to love, to share. This is a precious moment, but it is transient. It is a little parenthesis in eternity. If we share with caring, lightheartedness, and love, we will create abundance and joy for each other. And then this moment will have been worthwhile.
~ Deepak Chopra

WHAT YOU SEEK IS SEEKING YOU

The Lotus in the Mud

This book is like any other tool; it will work as much as you put it into practice. You will not be pushed into doing exercises or held accountable for following through with the actions presented in the materials. What I will say is this: you were led to my book for a reason. It is my intention to share my philosophy and experience to help you gain another perspective. I encourage you to go within, where all of the answers are waiting. This journey can be life-changing and transformational as long as you are willing to be honest with yourself that the habits, behaviors, and internal patterns that have been guiding you for many years, possibly even lifetimes, may not work. This can be a rewarding journey; when we learn to calm the mind, everything falls into place. The ideas presented here are the result of my own spiritual journey, and the willingness to understand the language my soul was trying to reveal.

Struggle for me was a daily experience, when stuck in a corporate job; experiencing crippling fear on a daily basis, not sleeping, not eating properly and having constant panic attacks. Like a lotus, growth stems from time in the mud. I had a "knowing" that change was necessary or my life was going to be in serious danger. I watched family members wrestle with panic and fear, mainly from money worries and a lack of self-love. Many died from various physical ailments, yet I feel the root cause was long term (chronic) stress, and ignoring the voice of their truth. I learned from my pain and loss, allowing my ancestors to become my "teachers," reminding me of what I was ready to release from my life.

My journey is my own and I reminded myself that I do not

need to repeat others' mistakes and wrong turns. I decided to take back my life, one deep breath at time, deciding not to walk the same path as much of my family had and slowly forged my own trail. I suspect you may be like me, questioning the path before you, and asking if it is your own or one that has been handed down to you to travel.

This journey relied upon my willingness to listen to the nudges from my spirit. A beautiful circumstance unfolded with my compliance, and the more I learned about my spiritual connection, the more comfort and safety began to wash over me, proving how natural it could be to live like this.... simply listening and acting upon that guidance. Ordinarily, many of us push, struggle, and force our particular agenda, whereas there is a beauty in allowing life to proceed unimpeded, welcoming us into the next transition with ease and grace; a gentle strengthening of our spiritual connection. I can guarantee one thing; you have a spirit and it will reach out you at all times and in multiple ways.

There may have been a moment when you had an awareness of this guidance, perhaps only after something took place that made you feel like you should've listened to or adhered to the signs. Let's make a pact right now to release the should've's, could've's, and would've's. Knowing better equates to doing better, and everything else is a learning opportunity. Hopefully you're still with me at this point, if so, rest in the awareness that you have everything you need already, there is nothing you need do or prepare, only allow yourself to accept what feels in alignment for you as you read through and absorb the messages within this book.

Imagine yourself successful. Always picture yourself successful. Visualize the person you desire to become. Set aside time each day to be alone and undisturbed. Get comfortable and relax. Close your eyes and concentrate on your desires and goals. See yourself in this new environment, capable and self-confident.

~ Napoleon Hill

TAKE A DEEP BREATH

Chapter 1

What is a Spiritual Nudge?

We each have a voice within; listening to it or dismissing it is a choice. Everyone experiences their soul or their higher self uniquely. You may have a feeling, while I experience a deep knowing. You may hear a voice from outside yourself, while I see in visuals. Perhaps you are inspired to take a different road home from work only to find out later that you avoided a terrible car accident. Maybe you have an awareness that your job is affecting your health. For many it can arrive in thought, like having an inspired idea to start eating better or to take that risk you've been thinking about, or begin writing that story the world needs you to share.

Although at times we can mistake our spiritual nudges for thoughts, there is a difference. The more you learn about yourself, and how to connect to the spirit within, the easier it will become to decipher what can often feel like code. I have come to understand the voice and messages from my own spirit as a nudge; not a push or form of control. Spirit does not manipulate us into a way or pathway, spirit simply creates the invitation for us to listen if we choose to follow the guidance provided.

We all have our own version of a nudge from spirit. Collectively we are receiving messages continuously, although at times it can seem as if nothing is happening or coming through. We need only adjust our means of reception to accept the message from the level it is being delivered to us. Receiving and experiencing guidance is unique to every individual. We will examine four main areas that are most common to our human design. Take notice of which ones you feel alignment with or those that come more naturally for you, as well as those areas in which you could use some practice. The four avenues we will be examining that allow us to receive guidance are known as the "clairs." As you journey through each of these "clairs," listen to your body, your mind, and your thoughts for each one. Pay attention to any resistance within your body. Maybe you feel a tingling sensation, a shift in temperature, images popping into your head, or even uneasiness about exploring the material in this book. This is completely normal; sometimes when we are about to experience something new or different it may challenge our beliefs about the world we live in and the capabilities of the human body. Read the following information with an open heart and mind and ask to receive what feels right for you. This is a beautiful journey of exploration, a discovery that can reveal magic and miracles. Magic is not for the naïve, young in age, or immature… magic is for those who believe in their hearts we are made of stardust laced with ancient wisdom and fueled by the potential to create our lives.

Whatever we are waiting for - peace of mind, contentment, grace, the inner awareness of simple abundance - it will surely come to us, but only when we are ready to receive it with an open and grateful heart.
~ Sarah Ban Breathnach

Self-Guided Spirit Session:

Take a moment to write out a spiritual experience you had from the past. This helped you recognize you were not alone, larger forces were at work, and there is more to this world/universe than meets the eye.

_____

_____

_____

_____

_____

_____

_____

_____

_____

_____

_____

_____

_____

_____

_____

_____

_____

_____

_____

_____

_____

_____

_____

What are some of the ways you connect with your spirit? If you are not sure, what are the hobbies, opportunities, or activities that bring you so much joy you "lose" time while doing them?

_____

_____

_____

_____

_____

_____

_____

_____

_____

_____

_____

_____

_____

_____

_____

_____

_____

_____

_____

_____

_____

_____

_____

_____

_____

_____

_____

_____

_____

_____

_____

_____

_____

_____

_____

_____

_____

_____

_____

_____

_____

_____

_____

_____

_____

_____

_____

_____

YOU
ARE
BRAVE
ENOUGH

Chapter 2

Clairaudience:
clear hearing/ clear listening

This clair is based on the auditory way of connecting. Think of anything audio, such as a radio voice, your own internal dialogue, and sound. There are unlimited avenues to experience clairaudience. My method of experiencing clairaudience felt so quiet and internal when it first began that I dismissed it or felt as if I were making it all up. My spiritual nudge sometimes showed up when I happened to overhear a select sentence from a nearby table in the coffee shop, or when I would ask a question and an answer would arise from within.

When I was considering moving, I kept asking over and over internally, "Should I move?" Sure enough, within a short time, I overheard "our moving here was the best choice we ever made," from a couple sipping their latte two tables over. Ten years ago, I would've dismissed that information, possibly not even have heard it from the couple sitting near me, most certainly not taking it as guidance. Very few of us are taught to pay attention to these intuitive experiences, I for one was not and when I naturally began to do so, they began occurring time and time again. I also did not have anyone to talk me through them or explain what was happening to me at the time. This generated fear and it took many years for me to rebuild trust in myself and spirit. As a result of much study, attending classes, self-evaluation, certifications, and retreats,

I have developed a strong connection built on this certainty of self I have discovered. I've gained clarity as I completed the work and committed to the path of getting in touch with my spirit and learning how my spirit speaks to me; then the signs became so much clearer and easier to see, feel, hear or know.

When I am in touch with my clairaudience, I might be listening to a song on the radio, but not really paying attention to the words, when all a sudden a word, phrase, or sentence stands out almost as if it is echoing in my mind. When this occurs, I pay attention to what was said and then sit with it in meditation because often I find it offers information or insight. Most likely it is the answer to a question, guidance for my next action steps, or possibly just a sweet reminder from a loved one who has passed on that they are still with me.

There are a variety of ways you can develop clairaudience; as you read through the next few sections, a particular "clair" might speak to you more than another. All of the clairs, are within our capacity to develop and strengthen; therefore, you may have greater strengths in one "clair" over another. As a certified hypnotherapist and life coach, I've become very good at listening to what's NOT being said. I read between the lines, and listen for the guidance of my own spirit when others are talking. Sometimes I can feel the energy and truth behind their words; other times I feel like something is missing, like they're not saying what they mean, or not including everything. Sometimes they're not even aware of how their spirit is sending guidance. Some of us have been taught that it's not okay to listen to ourselves and that we should seek counsel outside ourselves from other people. This is not my belief or how I operate in my life when it comes to intuition, although it is not good or bad, just my own, different path.

{Spiritual Nudge Wisdom Bit} To begin practicing, ask yourself how you hear and listen. When you hear sound, do you recognize a sensitivity to certain tones? Do you feel receptive to people's inflections? Do you often have to ask people to repeat themselves or to speak up? Have you ever had the experience of feeling like somebody called your name yet there's no one present? Do you hear noises from faraway that others can't hear? Do you sometimes hear music when there's no music playing?

Take some time to write down some of your responses here:

_____

_____

_____

_____

_____

_____

_____

_____

_____

_____

_____

_____

_____

_____

_____
_____
_____
_____
_____
_____
_____
_____
_____
_____
_____
_____
_____
_____
_____
_____
_____
_____
_____
_____
_____
_____
_____
_____
_____
_____

_____

_____

_____

_____

_____

_____

_____

_____

_____

_____

_____

_____

_____

_____

_____

_____

_____

_____

_____

_____

_____

_____

_____

_____

_____

Respond to every call that excites your spirit.

~ Rumi

Sound and clairaudience can be very subtle, and in my experience, they can lack logic, not making any sense in the moment. On some occasions, I've actually heard a low hum when I am in some physical locations, especially near the vortex sites in the city of Sedona, Arizona where I live. I also experience a sound like static that is not very clear, and almost barely audible, except for when the sound stops; then my senses become more alert and I pay attention to whatever words or actions I perceive in that moment.

Do not get discouraged if you're not connecting with the nudges of your spirit or with clairaudience, because you most likely have strengths in other areas; it is also possible you may not be used to tapping into your clairaudience. Sometimes the voice of spirit will sound like your own voice, coming through like you're talking to yourself when you are actually being guided by spirit. These are all possibilities, open to interpretation, and subject to your own experience. Of all the "clairs," clairaudience is one of the less common.

In my younger years, I was a bit of a rebel, often getting into situations that were dangerous. On one occasion, I was hanging out with a couple of friends in an area I knew we really shouldn't have been exploring, and in hindsight, I was with friends I probably should not have been with either. We were behind a stranger's home, walking through an alleyway when I heard a defining voice in my ear telling me to not go to the front of the house, and I dismissed it. At the same time I heard the voice, there was a flash in my mind of a police car. I walked to the front of the house and sure enough, there was a policeman escorting one of my friends into the back of the car. He had taken some garbage can lids off of the trash cans and was having fun using the lids like giant Frisbees, hurling them down the street. Luckily the officer knew my friend's uncle, so he gave us a little chat about being disrespectful then let us go on our way.

Even though I wasn't doing anything technically wrong, my spirit was trying to show me all that felt out of alignment, and when the voice didn't sound, I received the image in my mind. Clairaudience and clairvoyance were coming into play, but my stubborn ego at that time had no interest in listening to my spirit; for me, it was all about having fun and resisting authority.

Do you experience clairaudience:

- Do you learn better when you listen to someone describe the lesson?

- Do you say the phrase, "I hear what you are saying"?

- Do you hear tones, sounds, or even music that others cannot hear?

- Do you hear an internal voice (different then the ego), or a voice trying to get your attention?

- Do you sometimes hear the phone ring before it actually does?

- Do you connect with music? Are you able to separate the musical instruments in your mind as you listen?

- Do you talk to yourself?

- Do others like to tell you their life stories?

- Do you love to listen to the sounds of nature? Do they get louder and clearer the more time you spend outdoors?

- Do you feel sensitive to sounds, especially loud ones that make you jump but do not seem to bother others?

Take time to write down your responses here:

_____

_____

_____

_____

_____

_____

_____

_____

_____

_____

_____

_____

_____

_____

_____

_____

_____

_____

_____

_____

_____

_____

_____

_____

_____

_____

_____

_____

_____

_____

_____

_____

_____

_____

_____

_____

_____

_____

_____

_____

_____

_____

_____

_____

_____

_____

_____

_____

_____

_____

_____

_____

_____

_____

_____

_____

_____

_____

_____

_____

_____

_____

_____

_____

_____

_____

_____

_____

_____

_____

_____

*It takes courage to grow up and turn out to
be who you really are.*
~ E.E. Cummings

Ways to Develop Clairaudience:

1. Ask a friend to call you and chat about something they are struggling with. Listen very intently and notice if any words stand out to you, then repeat back to them what they are experiencing to show you are listening. This improves your listening skills while helping you understand if you are hearing people say what they really intend, instead of projecting your ideas onto them.

2. Go outside and sit quietly. Listen to the world around you. Do certain sounds seem closer or farther away? Do some sounds make you uncomfortable or do they bring you peace? Can you hear more profoundly when in nature than when you first began seeking clarity?

3. Play a piece of classical music. Close your eyes (this helps me when I am intuiting), and try to separate the various instruments in your mind. Do they blend together? Are you able to discern between them?

4. Spend a day listening to everyone you come in contact with. Try to stay present with what they are saying. What comes up for you? Do you have a hard time following what they tell you? Is it easier to hear one person over another? Try it in a group or public setting like a coffee shop and take notice of the conversations or sounds you are drawn to.

5. Write down the messages you hear internally, and ask yourself if it is the voice of the ego, or the voice of your spirit? Is it kind, friendly, and loving, or filled with judgment or blame?

Take time to write down your responses here:

_____

_____

_____

_____

_____

_____

_____

_____

_____

_____

_____

_____

_____

_____

_____

_____

_____

_____

_____

_____

_____

_____

_____

_____

_____

_____

_____

_____

_____

_____

_____

_____

_____

_____

_____

_____

_____

_____

_____

_____

_____

_____

_____

_____

_____

_____

_____

_____

*You must mentally accept in the present what
you actually want to happen in the future.
Picturing it brings the acceptance
much quicker.
~ Catherine Ponder*

Self-Guided Spirit Session:

Take a moment to close your eyes and follow the natural rhythm of your breath. Call in all of your senses simply by setting the intention to magnify them. Take five to ten deep breaths from this state of being. What do you notice?

_____

_____

_____

_____

_____

_____

_____

_____

_____

_____

_____

_____

_____

_____

_____

_____

_____

_____

Let's pretend spirit has a message for you in this very moment. Close your eyes, breath in deeply and ask to "hear" what you need to know. Write about your experience.

_____

_____

_____

_____

_____

_____

_____

_____

_____

_____

_____

_____

_____

_____

_____

_____

_____

_____

_____

_____

_____

_____

_____

Chapter #3

Clairsentience: clear feeling/touching

Clairsentience is sensing temperature, gut feelings, and physical reactions. You probably have heard people say it feels like their skin is crawling, or that they have butterflies in their stomach, both clairsentient statements. Of all the clairs, I believe clairsentience to be one of the most common gifts. Interestingly enough, it can also be the most difficult to understand. I connect clairsentience to being highly empathic, or sensitive, for those of us who feel it all! It was a challenge for me, most of my life, to understand what I was feeling, then describe it. Conveying it to others was another layer of the lesson.

Clairsentience is one of my stronger senses; when I was young and crazy, not listening to my spirit, I often ended up in situations that could've landed me in a lot of trouble...or worse. On one particular occasion, a friend stopped by with a carload of people. This was a common experience in my younger days, tons of people, tons of partying, tons of drugs, tons of alcohol, tons of everything. I had a sinking feeling in my stomach, a heaviness in my body as if everything within me was turning inward. My physical being felt weighed down, as if it were trying to tell me to pay attention. The words coming out of my friend's mouth did not line up with the energy I was feeling. Remember in the beginning when I described the friend who said, "I'm fine," in the introduction? This is an example of the importance of listening to your inner voice regardless of what you are hearing. My friend at the time (God rest his soul, a few years later he died because of his lifestyle) was trying to convince me to come along for a ride to get drugs. Although I had taken this trip many times before, something about this particular moment did not feel right and that sinking feeling got worse and worse.

Back then I wasn't good about standing in my power or speaking my truth, but thankfully on this day my spirit took over and I told them I wasn't feeling well and was staying home. Weeks later I found out what they did the day that I decided to stay home. They went into New York City and exchanged stolen guns for drugs. Each person in that car was later questioned for this incident, and I was grateful to have no part of it because I listened to my spirit. I'd like to say that was the end of the harsh lessons for me, but I'm stubborn. I needed the spiritual 2 x 4 instead of the tap on the shoulder. You may resonate with the idea of a sinking feeling with clairsentience. Feelings dictate our experience, such as how your body reacts when certain people speak to you, when around specific people, or when visiting different places. You might feel physical sensations and painful reactions; your body may become a spiritual antenna, picking up vibrations and energy that seem to they belong to you, although it could be from anyone around you or your conscious awareness. Do you pay attention to sensations within your body that are trying to tell you something is wrong or out of alignment? My spirit needed a variety of situations to grab my attention ... we can choose less intense lessons when we become sensitive to the messages we are given.

If you are clairsentient, you may have been guided to buy this book from how you felt when you first heard about it. Was there a knowing or a longing to check it out? Feelings can be overwhelming, especially when we feel lost or stuck when understanding emotions and feelings in a healthy way.

Unfortunately for many it has become a habit to suppress our emotions and feelings, storing them deep within, until the body itself begins to speak up. I believe I came into the world born as a clairsentient, and then as I evolved, that ability became enhanced by the experiences I had young in life. Growing up in a household that lacked a positive form of expression and seemed void of emotion altogether was confusing, and there was a lingering sadness in the air, like a thick heavy fog. My parents did the best they could, and tried to not fight in front of me and my siblings. Even though they had the best intentions, and wanted to keep us from feeling and experiencing their pain and struggles, I felt it all anyway. This sent a message to my body that my internal feelings did not make sense with what people were reflecting back to me. When this occurred, I quickly learned to dismiss my feelings and not trust myself. I was seeking external validation, an explanation or understanding of why what I was feeling internally did not line up with what was occurring externally. The truth is it did line up, but being young and not clear in what I was experiencing led me to feel there was something wrong with me, not the people hiding the truth.

{Spiritual Nudge Wisdom Bit} To begin practicing, ask yourself how you feel within the world around you. When you are out walking in nature do you feel overwhelmed with sensory information? Do you feel sensitive to your surroundings? Do you avoid talking to certain people because of the way they make you feel? Have you ever felt pain in your body that someone right next to you was also experiencing? Do you sense things that others can't? Do you sometimes have visceral reactions to things without an explanation why? Have you ever felt like something was "off" or not right about a situation?

Take time to write down your thoughts or responses here:

_____

_____

_____

_____

_____

_____

_____

_____

_____

_____

_____

_____

_____

_____

_____

_____

_____

_____

_____

_____

_____

_____

_____

_____

_____

_____

_____

_____

_____

_____

_____

_____

_____

_____

_____

_____

_____

_____

_____

_____

_____

_____

_____

_____

_____

_____

_____

_____

_____

_____
_____
_____
_____
_____
_____
_____
_____
_____
_____
_____
_____
_____
_____
_____
_____
_____
_____
_____
_____
_____
_____

How does one become a butterfly? You must want to fly so much that you are willing to give up being a caterpillar.

~ Trina Paulus

It took many years for me to regain trust in myself, even though my spirit was trying to prove me right all along. After studying the mind body and spirit for over 15 years, I finally developed an agreement with my spirit on how I receive my guidance. Clairsentience for me is very strong, and for the most part I know the difference between when I'm feeling something due to insight and awareness, or something from fear because a thought triggered an emotion. This discernment is crucial to learning how to trust in your abilities.

Practice in this area will help you gain awareness in those abilities, and how you connect to them. One of the most common traits of clairsentience is uncertainty if what you are experiencing is a true insight or intuition; or a fear or worry. When we are focused on what's in our heads it may feel heavy, dense, overactive, and fearful because we are following a thread of an emotion. The beauty of this is that you always have the ability to ask for clarity. If you're receiving a feeling, a message, or an insight, and you're not sure whether it's coming from ego, fear, or love, ask. Get in touch with the spirit aspect of yourself and ask for more clarity. There's nothing wrong with seeking help until you're able to discern more clearly for yourself.

Do you experience clairsentience?

- Do you experience clairsentience?

- Do you feel things happening in your body as people are talking to you?

- Do you notice temperature changes in a room?

- Can you feel when there has been an argument in a room you have just entered?

- Do you question why you are feeling something different than what someone is telling you is real?

- Do you ever get chills or goose bumps in specific situations?

- Do you avoid certain people or situations because you feel drained afterward?

- Do you have a sense of clutter and messiness? (Go within, make sure it stems from how it feels and not how it looks.)

- Have you been called overly sensitive?

- Do you change your mind easily based upon whom you associate with?

- Do you struggle in understanding where your energy ends and someone else's begins? (Energetically or in knowing who you are?)

Take time to write down your thoughts or responses here:

_____

_____

_____

_____

_____

_____

_____

_____

_____

_____

_____

_____

_____

_____

_____

_____

_____

_____

_____

_____

_____

_____

_____

_____

_____

_____

_____

_____

_____

_____

_____

_____

_____

_____

_____

_____

_____

_____

_____

_____

_____

_____

_____

_____

_____

_____

_____

_____

_____

Ways to help you develop clairsentience:

1. Watch a TV show and try to figure out how the show will end. Pay attention to how certain characters make you feel, whether you gravitate towards them or feel repelled by them.

2. Write random sentences and affirmations down on paper. Place those notes inside envelopes. Make sure you have a mix of positive and negative statements/affirmations. Hold each one in your hands and then write down how you feel when holding the envelope; do not open until you have gone through each one. Open to compare your feelings after holding each envelope.

3. Draw an outline of your body on paper. Take colored pencils and color, mark, write, what physical pain or sensations you have in certain areas. Then decide what emotions are trapped within those pain areas. Give them a voice, and let them out.

4. Practice noticing how you feel around certain people, situations, and locations. Do you feel energized or weighed down? Do you feel excited to talk to some people, and uncomfortable with others?

5. Hold various objects in your hands, then try to describe what you feel and if there is a story to those objects. Have a friend provide a selection of items for you to practice with.

Take time to write down your thoughts or responses here:

_____

_____

_____

_____

_____

_____

_____

_____

_____

_____

_____

_____

_____

_____

_____

_____

_____

_____

_____

_____

_____

_____

_____

_____

_____

_____

_____

_____
_____
_____
_____
_____
_____
_____
_____
_____
_____
_____
_____
_____
_____
_____
_____
_____
_____
_____
_____
_____
_____
_____

*Sitting quietly, doing nothing, spring comes,
and the grass grows by itself.*
~ Zen Proverb

Self-Guided Spirit Session:

Take a moment to close your eyes and follow the natural rhythm of your breath. Sit in stillness and really feel your body. Notice the sensations, muscles, temperature changes, etc. What did you notice?

_____

_____

_____

_____

_____

_____

_____

_____

_____

_____

_____

_____

_____

_____

_____

_____

_____

_____

Let's pretend spirit has a message for you in this very moment. Close your eyes, breathe in deeply and ask to "feel" what you need to know. Write about your experience.

_____

_____

_____

_____

_____

_____

_____

_____

_____

_____

_____

_____

_____

_____

_____

_____

_____

_____

_____

_____

GET
QUIET
GO.
WITHIN

Chapter #4

Clairvoyance: clear seeing/clear sight

Clairvoyance is vision, seeing internally within the mind's eye as well as externally. A few years back I questioned my desire to move a few hours north of where we currently lived. I knew that this move would affect my job, my friendships, my son's entire known way of life, as well as my husband's personal and business life. I was constantly weighing the benefits, the risks, my fears, my husband's concerns, my son's resistance... and the list goes on. One day while driving I decided to ask for help. I said a silent prayer, asking for clarity and guidance. Less than a minute later sitting at a traffic light I casually glanced up at the license plate of the car in front of me. "Go north," was clearly displayed on the license plate, practically screaming at me! I began to laugh and cry at the same time. The secret to receiving this message for me, was first asking, being present enough to pay attention, then trusting, not second-guessing the message. It is so easy to discredit the message when we want to control the source it comes in from.

Clairvoyance is understanding that your vision goes beyond the use of your physical eyes. Seeing outside of yourself through your eyes is only one aspect of clairvoyance. There's a misbelief that a clairvoyant message or sign needs to come from a glowing magical angel or spiritual being. Not that it doesn't show up that way for some, although it can be much subtler and often is.

In my personal experience with clairvoyance I receive an internal image, from my mind's eye, almost like there's a little window that pops up and I see an image, a movie, or series of images. Once in a while I have to close my eyes to see more clearly, while other times it just appears within. When I receive messages from my spirit, it often will arrive in images. I then decipher these images to determine if they are metaphors or symbols. I have learned the language of my own soul, developed over many years of trying to understand and interpret the information coming in. It isn't necessary for me to share those symbols or metaphors in this book simply because each person can experience vastly different correlations; what you may interpret as personal to you will not resonate with someone else and vice versa. Clairvoyance is not necessarily about what you are seeing, yet the negative layers, filters, and barriers may get in the way of your having clear sight. Many of us fear clairvoyance; of the clairs, this is the one I hear the most commonly that people are afraid to see. When we get into fear, we naturally block our insight and guidance. That doesn't mean it can't reach us, though it sure can make it difficult.

As a professional photographer, I can say my camera has saved my life. It opened other worlds, visions, and life's beauty to me in new ways. The camera helped me to see the light within other people, it guided me to walk them through a journey from head into heart. Although it is one of my gifts and how I help serve others, my clients also serve me. They have helped open my eyes to my own inner beauty. I recognize the light within me reflecting back from them. This to me is clairvoyance at its best, when healing and transformation are a result of seeing clearly and with love.

We all have layers of filters, perceptions and limiting beliefs that can block us from our own truth. This life can be an adventure of discovering them, one by one, releasing and removing those layers with ease, grace, and trust. A wonderful mentor of mine once said we can choose to remove the Band-Aid or we can allow the universe to rip the Band-Aid off for us. The way I take this is that sometimes in life we try to hide from what we don't want to see, so we run away or we fear that we're going to uncover unexpected darkness. My belief is that any darkness that may exist within...we are fully capable of handling. Each of us has a shadow side, an opportunity to explore your being to unleash an untapped beautiful potential. Clairvoyance is an invitation to reveal the areas of life that have not been apparent within your visibility.

There are various levels of clairvoyance, some enable one be clearly see into the present moment while others are able to venture into the past or the future. Your point of power is in the now. Clairvoyance can assist us by revealing lessons and guidance available within stories from the past. If you haven't learned something the first time around, exploring the patterns that have repeated in this life or other lifetimes can generate healing and create change. Transformation begins with awareness; the more aware you are the more you can move forward and take action, trusting in your spirit.

{Spiritual Nudge Wisdom Bit} To begin practicing, ask yourself how you see the world around you. When out walking in nature do you take in the beauty of the scenery? Do you see beyond your surroundings? Do you see lights, colors, or other visuals? Do you close your eyes to see within? Do you have vivid dreams with symbols and colors? Can you see a finished project in your mind before completing it?

Take time to write down your thoughts or responses here:

_____

_____

_____

_____

_____

_____

_____

_____

_____

_____

_____

_____

_____

_____

_____

_____

_____

_____

_____

_____

_____

_____

_____
_____
_____
_____
_____
_____
_____
_____
_____
_____
_____
_____
_____
_____
_____
_____
_____
_____
_____
_____
_____
_____
_____
_____
_____
_____
_____

_____

_____

_____

_____

_____

_____

_____

_____

_____

_____

_____

_____

_____

_____

_____

_____

_____

_____

_____

_____

_____

_____

_____

*You can have anything you want if you are
willing to give up the belief that you
can't have it.*

~ Robert Anthony

Clairvoyance includes signs & symbols, seeing words appear in thin air, or anything else that grabs your attention with the physical eye. Noticing billboards and license plates is actually quite common for many people but not everyone believes them to be. Discerning messages and taking action on them results in exceptional outcomes. Cultivating trust is crucial, in yourself and in spirit. Clairvoyance can be tricky since it is a visual ability; you must be present enough to recognize what you are seeing as a message compared to picking up on a judgment. For example, when seeing a homeless person walk down the street, you may get a sense of sadness and fear, yet you need to recognize it as either your own sadness and fear, or because you are witnessing someone else's sorrow. Although there is a fine line here, my philosophy is that people become mirrors for us. When I tap into claircognizance and clairvoyance, I make a decision to receive information that is relevant for a specific individual or situation, not my judgment about them. Noticing a person carrying a red bag is an awareness, while questioning their outfit or accessory choice is a judgment. Having an awareness of is different from giving feedback based on that awareness.

Do you experience clairvoyance?

- Do you experience clairvoyance?

- Do you learn best by watching someone do what they are teaching you?

- Do you see images in your mind's eye when reading or telling a story?

- Do you notice details in your environment that others do not?

- Do you notice lights or shadows that fade quickly when you bring them to your attention?

- Can you visually see beauty or potential in a home's decor or piece of furniture?

- Do you like to color, paint, or take photos?

- Do you have a visceral reaction to certain images or movies?

- Is it hard for you to "see" things in life?

- When you were younger did you have a special friend that only you could see?

- Do you see energy or colors around people, places, animals, or plants?

Take time to write down your thoughts or responses here:

_____

_____

_____

_____

_____

_____

_____

_____

_____

_____

_____

_____

_____

_____

_____

_____

_____

_____

_____

_____

_____

_____

_____

_____

Ways to develop clairvoyance:

1. Play with a camera, perhaps the one in your phone. Go outside and find ten things you are drawn to photograph. Ask your spirit what the image seems to convey to you.

2. Look to the clouds, water, or mountaintops. What do you see? Does something take form or shape to become a message?

3. Pay attention to license plates, billboards, nature, animals, etc. Is there a message for you?

4. Practice seeing with your internal mind; ask for clarity from your spirit. Ask to be shown what you need to "see."

5. Play with a word find; this is an excellent way to sharpen your sight and to learn if certain words pop off of page for you.

Take time to write down your thoughts or responses here:

_____

_____

_____

_____

_____

_____

_____

_____

_____

_____

_____

_____

_____

_____

_____

_____

_____

_____

_____

_____

_____

_____

_____

_____

_____
_____
_____
_____
_____
_____
_____
_____
_____
_____
_____
_____
_____
_____
_____
_____
_____
_____
_____
_____
_____
_____

Keep your face towards the sunshine and shadows will fall behind you.
~ Walt Whitman

Self-Guided Spirit Session:

Close your eyes and follow the natural rhythm of your breath. Imagine seeing a beautiful space within your mind. Allow visuals to come into your scope of vision with your eyes closed. Does it have color, texture, a location or color? What did you notice?

_____

_____

_____

_____

_____

_____

_____

_____

_____

_____

_____

_____

_____

_____

_____

_____

_____

_____

_____

_____

Let's pretend spirit has a message for you in this very moment. Close your eyes, breathe in deeply and ask to "see" what you need to know. Write about your experience.

_____

_____

_____

_____

_____

_____

_____

_____

_____

_____

_____

_____

_____

_____

_____

_____

_____

_____

_____

_____

_____

YOU
ARE
MORE
Powerful
Then
You
Realize

Chapter #5

Claircognizance:
clear knowing/understanding

Knowing information, tapping in to accurate insight without knowing where it came from or how you received it is claircognizance. During my mind, body, and spirit training, early on I discovered claircognizance. In client after client, I could sense their pain, relationship status, emotional baggage, and desires. They would often open up after a short time with me, sharing their fears and darkest secrets. My soul nudged me to pay attention and acknowledge this occurrence, to stop talking myself out of what I was receiving. I would spend maybe five or ten extra minutes massaging a wrist to find out the client had a previous injury there and it had just flared up on them that morning. Other times it was a shoulder, the low back, and time and time again they would ask me, "How did you know I had that pain? I forgot to mention it when I filled out the paperwork." Claircognizance was a new sense for me; many of my clairs were still being developed at this time, and continue to improve to this day. This feeling came so naturally to me that I didn't even realize it was anything extraordinary, acquiring a result lacking vision, hearing, or thought, just a knowing that felt so close to my own awareness that I wasn't able to discern that it was actually guidance.

This is one of the challenges with claircognizance; it can feel so simple and natural, it seems to have been with you all along, when really that knowing just entered into your experience. You may encounter someone and instantly know random facts about them that you could've sworn they told you, yet the information entered into your mind without prior insight. Sometimes the information enters into the experience like an idea popping into your head, or an awareness that floats to the surface in your mind. For others it appears as an answer you have confidence in, and a knowing fed to you by your guide or your spirit.

Claircognizance can be challenging considering the profound level of trust some of us need for acceptance. At some point, each of us have engaged in making poor choices. For some of us this has led to a disconnect from spirit, challenging our ability to make good decisions or listen to sound judgment. Claircognizant messages will be dismissed if we are lacking belief and trust in ourselves. I highly recommend examining how you talk to yourself, looking within to strengthen your self-esteem and confidence.

I remember how uncomfortable I was to recognize my "knowing"; sometimes it was very different from what other people could understand. I recall a situation when my knowing made someone so uncomfortable that I decided I was wrong and felt great shame towards myself. A friend of the family witnessed me sharing something they didn't believe an eight-year-old child would know, and it changed how she viewed me. We became distanced from moment on. I am sure many of you can relate to what it feels like to have someone try to dismiss, ignore, or devalue your gifts, especially when it is connected to a form of expression. This is crucial in childhood, and an important part of learning how we fit in and navigate through this world. Small moments can change how someone shows up in their space, it can shift how they communicate and express themselves. It also is the reason many of us have shut down our intuitive abilities and connection to our spirits.

{Spiritual Nudge Wisdom Bit} To begin practicing, ask yourself if you have random thoughts floating through your mind? Do you feel a fluidity within your mind that you trust? Do you "know" beyond your conscious awareness? Does it seem people provide you with information they say they didn't? Do you always find a solution to a problem? Can you put facts together very quickly?

Take time to write down your thoughts or responses here:

_____

_____

_____

_____

_____

_____

_____

_____

_____

_____

_____

_____

_____

_____

_____

_____

_____

_____

_____

_____

_____

_____

_____

_____

_____

_____

_____

_____

_____

_____

_____

_____

_____

_____

_____

_____

Claircognizance can be having the right words or knowing what actions to take, because it simply popped into your mind. Premonitions (a strong feeling, vision, or knowing that something is about to happen) are forms of claircognizance and the other clairs. A premonition can provide insight to where, when, and who will be involved, without prior knowledge of any of the aspects. Deja vu is an example of this phenomenon, and with claircognizance it can be an extremely potent feeling of having known something or having had an experience before.

Claircognizance can defeat logic and knowledge, leaving you surprised with how accurate your feelings were when others were certain they were right. Hindsight always makes it easier to recognize claircognizant abilities. After an incident or issue occurs to which we know we should say no, we often second-guess ourselves and override our good judgment. This happens a lot in my industry, colleagues have a feeling that they shouldn't move forward with a project, circumstance, or individual, yet they talk themselves out of listening to the guidance and then have a more difficult circumstance to deal with as a result.

Do you experience claircognizance?

- Do you experience claircognizance?

- Do you often know the answer to a question without knowing how?

- Do you receive messages, relevant ideas, or solutions that pop into your mind?

- Do you know when someone is telling the truth or being dishonest?

- Do you experience premonitions?

- Do you have knowledge about people, places, or things that feels like it has "been" with you without your awareness as to how?

- Have you ever received insight or an understanding of something without prior knowledge of it?

- Have you had an answer appear without having prior knowledge or background on it?

- Have you looked back at a situation and recognized you knew what to do but just didn't act upon it?

- Do you often receive inspired ideas seemingly from nowhere?

- Were you ever labeled a "know-it-all" when you were younger (or now)?

Take time to write down your thoughts or responses here:

_____
_____
_____
_____
_____
_____
_____
_____
_____
_____
_____
_____
_____
_____
_____
_____
_____
_____
_____
_____
_____

*The creation of a thousand forests is
in one acorn.*

~Ralph Waldo Emerson

Ways to help you develop Claircognizance:

1. Try automatic writing, to receive information without forcing it.

2. Ask a question, then meditate on it. Does the answer appear in your mind?

3. Begin paying attention to your thoughts and exploring when and where you receive them. Consider keeping a journal to document each experience.

4. Set your intention for angels, guides, or spirit to provide you with information. Go for a walk in nature; notice if you received anything significant after your walk is complete.

5. Have someone hide objects in your home; do you feel guided to locate them with thoughts or ideas that come into your mind.

Take time to write down some thoughts or responses here:

_____

_____

_____

_____

_____

_____

_____

_____

_____
_____
_____
_____
_____
_____
_____
_____
_____
_____
_____
_____
_____
_____
_____
_____
_____
_____
_____
_____
_____
_____
_____
_____
_____
_____

Just as ripples radiate from the place where a stone is thrown into a pool of water, our sometime-unconscious thoughts, feelings, emotions, and beliefs create the "disturbances" in the Field that become the blueprints for our lives.

~ Gregg Braden

Self-Guided Spirit Session:

Take a moment to close your eyes and follow the natural rhythm of your breath. Pretend there is a person visible into your mind's eye. Notice if they are gesturing to you, or nudging you to take an action. What did you perceive?

_____

_____

_____

_____

_____

_____

_____

_____

_____

_____

_____

_____

_____

_____

_____

_____

_____

Let's pretend spirit has a message for you. Close your eyes, breath in deeply and ask to "know" what you need to understand in this moment. Write about your experience.

_____

_____

_____

_____

_____

_____

_____

_____

_____

_____

_____

_____

_____

_____

_____

_____

_____

_____

_____

_____

ASK YOUR SPIRIT FOR GUIDANCE

Chapter #6

Higher Self & Spirit vs. The Mind

Deciphering between the constant chatter of the mind and the wisdom of the spirit can be daunting and confusing. Especially if it is new for you to connect with this aspect of yourself. When you are aware of behaviors and reactions, you become more in touch with the subtle differences between the ego/mind and the spirit. It is crucial that we are gentle with ourselves in this process. Just like anything else, learning how to get in touch with your spirit involves practice. You wouldn't go to the gym one time and expect to have perfectly toned muscles. Practice discipline and patience with yourself.

The voice of the spirit is never fearful. It will never shame you, make you feel guilty, or punish you in any way. The ego, on the other hand, will be filled with the voices of shouldn't, couldn't, and blame. The ego is very good at reminding us of why we will not succeed. It is important to understand the part of the human nervous system within the brain known as the lizard brain. The lizard brain has a very specific role, to keep you alive, and to keep you from harm and danger. The problem with the lizard brain is it does not know the difference between a true threat or an imagined or perceived threat. A true threat would be a hot stove; the lizard brain would keep you from placing your hand on a hot stove. An imagined threat would mask itself as failure. Let's pretend for a moment that you were inspired with a wonderful idea for your business. Now imagine that as you begin the planning process, all of a

Reptilian Brain

sudden you become overwhelmed with fear. You start thinking about all the ways you could fail. Into your mind enters thoughts of becoming homeless and losing it all. You go from an inspired business idea, to sudden failure in the blink of an eye. Your spirit was the inspired idea; your ego was the part that wants to say you would fail at achieving it.

Our spirits love us deeply and truly, and the guidance of the Spirit will never be filled with fear. Even if a business idea is not meant for us, and we ask for guidance from our spirit, we would never be guided with fear. We may be guided to a different way, a different opportunity, or to sit with the pros and cons. In the evaluation of the pros and cons, there may be more guidance from spirit, such as having too many cons over pros. The guidance will not be harsh, and it will never be self-critical. The self-criticism comes from within us and is the voice of our ego. Remember that funky little lizard brain we were talking about? It is reminding us of perceived threats, not inspired actions.

Ego

The ego has a wonderful way of trying to talk us out of taking action, pursuing dreams, crushing hopes, and staying small in our own lives. You can go from inspired thinking to questioning everything instantly, if you listen to the ego. It takes practice to soften the impact the mind and ego can have on you. Over time you will witness the tricks your mind tries to play, through mindfulness and a level of detachment from your own thoughts. If you have not tried meditation, I highly recommend it, it seriously changed my life. If you have tried meditation and did not connect with it, don't give up; try it again or find a style of meditation that works for you.

{Spiritual Nudge Wisdom Bit} Our outer world is a reflection of our inner world. Take a moment to connect with your breath, noticing how you breathe without trying to control it. Your breath can teach you about life, how you respond and resist change. Begin to take in more air with a slower, guided inhalation, followed by holding the breath for a few seconds, then a slow and steady releasing exhale. Repeat this for a round of three to five breaths. This is a great way to bring meditation in without having to go into complete solitude. I have practiced this while sitting in traffic, watching television, and as I write.

Take time to write down your thoughts or responses here:

_____

_____

_____

_____

_____

_____

_____

_____

_____

_____

_____

_____

_____

_____

_____

_____

_____

_____

_____

_____

_____

_____

_____

_____

_____

_____

_____

_____

_____

_____

_____

_____

_____

_____

_____

_____

_____

Everything is ok in the end, if it's not ok, then it's not the end.

~ Unknown

Your role in trusting yourself is crucial to the process of following through on spirit-given messages. If somewhere within your subconscious mind there is a pattern of self-sabotage, you may not listen to the voice of your spirit as loudly as you will your self-defeating behavior. Your spirit is always speaking to you, it's just a matter of releasing the layers that are in the way of your hearing it.

Think of your spirit and your guidance as light. Now imagine that there is a beautiful light within you. If you kept throwing blankets over the light, the light would still be there, although it would be extremely difficult to see clearly. Sometimes we have to peel back the layers in order to find our own light. The beautiful thing is in this lifetime there are always going to be more layers; at the same time we can move into a place of experiencing layers and our light in harmony with each other. The more you listen and set your intention to hear spirit, the louder it becomes when reaching you. This doesn't mean loud in tone or volume; this means more avenues become available to allow it to meet you where you are.

The clairs can deepen your life experience, serving as a way to gain clarity on the contrast between your mind and your spirit. If you are drawn to working with any particular clair, begin with what you already have within reach. For example, tuning in to clairsentience or clear feeling, you have the ability to start tapping into the "feeling" aspect when it comes to deciphering between the mind and spirit. One of my favorite simple exercises is placing your hand over your heart, and asking your higher self for clarity. Ask yourself, "What is my truth?", and notice if you receive any feelings or messages. On the journey of learning self-love and self-confidence, struggle is often present when receiving positive words directed towards yourself. Answers are available to you in any given moment, the key is learning to be open enough to receive them.

*Never give up on something that you can't go
a day without thinking about.
~ Unknown*

Higher Self & Spirit vs. The Mind Exercise:

(You will need a piece of paper and pen for this exercise)

1. Draw a line down the center of your paper, dividing the paper into two halves.

2. At the top of the left-hand side of the paper, write the word "Ego"

3. At the top of the right-hand side of the paper, write the word "Spirit"

4. On the left-hand side of the paper begin to write sentences that represent your fear, worry, and stress (i.e. I'm afraid I will never have enough money)

5. Make sure that you have written a minimum of ten sentences

6. Place your hand over your heart, close your eyes, and take five deep long breaths. Inhale the feelings of peace and calm, release or exhale any tension, worry, or fear.

7. Go to the right side of your paper, the section labeled "Spirit." Now write a positive statement to answer in truth (from your spirit). Each statement will be a message that speaks to the mind's sentences.

8. Trust in the process, at first it can feel like you're making it all up. The truth is, even if you are making it all up, it still works. (You are not making it up, you are just learning to connect with your spirit.)

Take time to write down your thoughts or responses here:

_____

_____

_____

_____

_____

_____

_____

_____

_____

_____

_____

_____

_____

_____

_____

_____

_____

_____

_____

_____

_____

_____

_____

_____

_____

_____

_____

_____

_____

_____

_____

_____

_____

_____

_____

_____

_____

_____

_____

_____

_____

_____

_____

_____

_____

_____

_____

_____

_____

_____

FACE YOUR FEARS

One of the most important facets to this exercise is noticing how you feel afterwards. How does it feel to release fear and worry? Are you trusting your spirit to answer them? Repeat this exercise as often as needed, allowing divine timing to be perfect.

As long as we are in a human body we will encounter challenges and growth opportunities; and while knowing this you also have a choice in how you respond to your feelings. You are divinely supported with the capacity to ask for clarity to reveal all the answers that reside within you. The next step is to let go of trying to figure it all out. You are operating from your head, not trusting in yourself by trying to figure it out.

We are unlimited beings with potential to create with the intention of our minds. For many of us, life experiences have taught us otherwise. At some point in time there may have been trauma, illness, or the loss of a loved one. Emotions become stirred, often leading to our questioning the purpose of such events. At the root of it all, we are love, deserving of love, and sometimes forget how to receive love. A direct connection exists between receiving love and receiving the messages of spirit: the gentle feeling of the wind against your cheek, the smell of the rose, and the laughter of a child. All of these things can be messages from spirit, if we allow ourselves to open up and receive them in that way.

One of the ways you can tune in to the voice of your spirit is to be in a place of gratitude. Gratitude magnifies all the things you are grateful for. When we are stressed and anxious it can be easy to forget how much we really have. Shifting attention to blessings changes the emotional state and reaction. Next time you feel stressed or fearful, focus upon the blessings in your life. A beautifully powerful and simple blessing is being grateful for the air that flows in and out of your lungs. Maybe that blessing is a warm sweater, helping you feel more comfortable during the winter months. Perhaps a cool glass of water, on a hot summer day. The only separation between you and the blessings in your life is your perception of the layers between them.

If you knew who walked beside you at all times on this path that you have chosen, you could never experience fear or doubt again.

~ Dr. Wayne Dyer

Self-Guided Spirit Session:

Close your eyes and follow the natural rhythm of your breath. Invite your heart to have a conversation with yourself. Ask your heart how it can help you feel more at peace. What did you receive?

freedom, respite, activity

Give the mind a few moments to ramble, release complaints, and write about fear, worry, or problems that come to the surface. Can you see the difference between the heart and the mind in your writing?

_____

_____

_____

_____

_____

_____

_____

_____

_____

_____

_____

_____

_____

_____

_____

_____

_____

_____

_____

_____

_____

Chapter #7

Grounding & Presence

Grounding is vital for listening to spirit and quieting the mind. As a meditation teacher, I find value in teaching grounding techniques. There are a variety of methods, and you may already have some fantastic ones of your own. My definition of grounding is knowing where my energy, focus, and attention are being placed all while maintaining my connection to the present moment. When you are present you are also in your body. The clairs are more efficient when you are in touch with the present moment. How can you feel sensations or receive messages from your body if you're not listening to it? How can you hear the voice of spirit if you're preoccupied with worry and fear in your mind? How can you see the beauty around you when you are distracted buy your cell phone or computer? Although we are spiritual beings, we are in human form. This human form consists of a nervous system, one of the beautiful bridges between the spirit world and your physical form. The body helps us to connect, and the more often we stay in the present moment the easier it will become.

Grounding techniques are taught from a variety of backgrounds and cultures. As a certified yoga teacher and shamanic practitioner, I have explored many methods, some involve the postures of yoga and others use the mind and imagination to visualize. Personally, because I am clairvoyant, I love the visual aspect of things. I'm also clairsentient, so I love to feel sensations as I go through the process. Seeing the images internally, while feeling the sensation physically, is my indicator that I am shifting into a grounded state. On a side note, many people drawn to the healing arts, metaphysics, and spirituality struggle with the term being "grounded." For some, the word grounded can sound like the opposite of light and playful; and playing in the realm of spirit feels light and free, so if you resonate with this idea you may not want to use the word "grounded," but "present" instead.

Connecting with the elements and the earth comes naturally to me. I like to smudge myself when doing so. If you're not familiar with that term, it's simply using sage or other plants to create smoke, then using that smoke to clear energy and spaces. After I practice smudging I feel lighter, clearer, and I tend to feel very grounded and present. Having the sunlight upon my face, and my feet on the earth (usually barefoot), is a sure way to bring me into my body, and into a focused state of awareness. Sometimes, I sit on the ground and lean against a tree, then I feel my energy going down into the tree, deep down into the earth and connecting with the core of the earth. I like to imagine roots coming from my body down into the earth, sometimes standing and other times sitting. This is an internal process; my eyes are closed and I'm imagining the roots moving downward. Sometimes there is a sensation, almost like magnets are on my feet gently pulling me down. None of these things are fearful, or create anxiety, yet again I remind you to find what works for you.

{Spiritual Nudge Wisdom Bit} Try experimenting with visualization by utilizing different elements, colors, textures, and aspects. Visualization can include the other senses such as feeling, hearing, and sensing throughout the visualization. You can imagine different environments as well, bringing variety to your experience.

Take time to write down your thoughts or responses here:

_____

_____

_____

_____

_____

_____

_____

_____

_____

_____

_____

_____

_____

_____

_____

_____

_____

_____

_____

_____

_____

_____

_____

_____
_____
_____
_____
_____
_____
_____
_____
_____
_____
_____
_____
_____
_____
_____
_____
_____
_____
_____
_____
_____
_____

Never tell me the sky is the limit when there are footprints on the moon.

~ Unknown

You will read the word presence over and over again as we explore its importance when tuning in to spirit. Your point of power is happening right now, it is not in the future. Every thought we think has its own vibration, and thoughts are like magnets attracting things to them. You may have heard of the law of attraction; a foundational belief everything is vibration first. If we are thinking too far into the future, or are being ruled by the past we are not living up to our potential. We have the power to create change, yet that change begins with the thoughts you are thinking right now. Do not beat yourself up mentally for less than perfect thoughts, the goal is to be honest about how we are feeling and to give the emotion and energy behind those thoughts a way out of the body and your experience.

Identifying your thoughts and discovering where they are coming from helps you begin to change them. Affirmations are one way to begin to move that energy into a positive space. At first you will feel as if you are lying to yourself, yet your subconscious mind is listening. Practice makes perfect; over time it will become easier and easier to accept loving and kind words. Creating an affirmation for yourself is a powerful way to embrace positive thinking. Practice taking time every single day to start reprogramming new positive thoughts. One day, after lots of practice, you will notice there's a little less resistance. Less resistance means you are moving with the flow, and moving with the flow equals connection to your spirit.

Our body is our greatest Oracle.

~ Sunny Dawn Johnston

Self-Guided Spirit Session:

Close your eyes and follow the natural rhythm of your breath. How many breaths do you need before you can feel a little more grounded? Try a two-minute, four-minute, and a six-minute breathing session. How did your body and mind respond to each one?

_____

_____

_____

_____

_____

_____

_____

_____

_____

_____

_____

_____

_____

_____

_____

_____

_____

_____

_____

Do you know what takes your mind out of the present moment? What is one thing you can do today to be more present and grounded throughout your day?

_____

_____

_____

_____

_____

_____

_____

_____

_____

_____

_____

_____

_____

_____

_____

_____

_____

_____

_____

_____

_____

Chapter #8

Creating Sacred Space

Sacred space is another important factor for connecting to spirit. If you do not feel safe in your environment, wherever that may be, your work, home, or otherwise, it can be difficult to hear the voice of your spirit. It is not necessary to have a special place where you only connect with your spirit, although you can; it is more important to have the intention to begin the process. Sacred space can be a room, it can be within your car, or a beautiful place outdoors; as long as it feels good to you.

The ultimate goal is to learn to create sacred space within yourself so that you may carry it with you everywhere you go. For me, my home is sanctuary. I have a room where I sleep and it's also the same room where I meditate and write my books. It's filled with the beautiful light from my salt lamp, a gentle scent of incense in the air, and I'm surrounded by all of my spiritual tools. Sometimes my sacred space is also sitting on my front porch, with its mountain views and the songs of the birds, I feel completely at peace. Sacred space can be fluid for you, it does not have to be only one area where you go. If you are more comfortable having one place as your sacred space, that is fine too. In sanctuary, it is important you try to keep the energy clear. You may smudge to clear the space. Keep it free of clutter to have it feel amazing every time you step into it. Let this be your go-to place when you need to be recharged, when you need healing, or a moment to get out of your head.

Some items I like to have in my sacred space, aside from the salt lamp and incense, are card decks, stones, classical music, and spiritual items. I have a feather, affirmations, and a gratitude journal I write in. What speaks to you? What items or objects make you feel loved and supported? You may have an image of a spiritual teacher, a loved one, or a mentor; a statue of a deity, a god or goddess, whatever speaks to you and reflects your personal beliefs. I work with the elements so sometimes I have different tools to represent each: fire, water, air, & earth.

Altars are beautiful additions to a sacred space. Altars can take up the entire room or even just a tiny space on the shelf. The important thing is how you feel when you see the items in your sacred space. An altar can hold space to represent anything you're trying to bring into your life or to enhance and magnify an energy you want to create. Some people have altars for prosperity, for a loved one who is transitioning, and for any other reason you could possibly imagine. I currently have an altar for the element fire because I am teaching an online course about the elements and moon cycles. The fire altar can help transform energy, assisting me in shifting from old patterns into new ways of being. Explore playing with altars, try different elements, colors, textures, images, tools; use your imagination and dive deep into your creativity.

Altars remind me of what's important in a particular moment in my life. Fresh flowers on my altar remind me to cultivate self-love; every time I see the flowers I am reminded to check-in with myself. I ask myself what are the thoughts I'm thinking, and are they in alignment with what I want to create? If the answer is no, then there's a possibility that I need to reevaluate and become a little bit more disciplined in my thinking. Sometimes the discipline comes in the form of being kind to myself. It doesn't need to be harsh or strict, it can be loving. Altars anchor energy to a space, creating a bridge for the earth and spirit to meet.

{Spiritual Nudge Wisdom Bit} Write out five different components of desired results you would like to experience from having an altar. Take those five things and decide what could represent them in physical form on your altar. Get creative and expand your mind when putting your altar together.

Take time to write down your thoughts or responses here:

_____

_____

_____

_____

_____

_____

_____

_____

_____

_____

_____

_____

After you have created a sacred space, ask yourself the following: How does it feel when I am in this space? Do I feel calm and grounded, at peace and able to tap into my spirit? Do I feel scattered, nervous, and uncertain? There is a difference between entering your sacred space with those emotions, or having those emotions surface from the space itself. Sacred space can help you process emotions, exploring why they are surfacing to begin with. Notice if you went to your sacred space feeling calm then once in it, started to feel agitated, or something other than calm and relaxed. This is why it's also very important to be present, so you can tell the difference when you shift from an emotion or feeling.

Sacred space can nurture your desires, and bring a sense of safety and peace into your life. If you feel agitated or annoyed or any other lower vibrational feelings, ask your spirit for clarity. Perhaps your sacred space is helping you to heal these emotions, and getting clarity can help you discern what it means for you. Every now and then, freshen it up a little, even if you keep all of the same items in your sanctuary. Explore moving them around to free things up and to invite fresh energy into the space. It is important to reevaluate your sacred area and your altar to make sure your items are in alignment with who you are and where you are heading. If something doesn't feel right to you it may be time for you to remove it; it's possible it may have served its purpose for you.

Have fun creating your sacred space, let it give you a feeling of joy. Do not get caught up in your mind questioning if you're doing it correctly, because then you are in your head and not allowing your spirit to guide you. Sometimes we may not know why we choose the objects or the places that we do, just trust in your spirit to lead you to the right place, and the perfect object for your individual altar. In Feng Shui, oftentimes people naturally place the things they need in their environment without even knowing the general rules or principles. This goes to show that if you listen to your spirit, everything will align at just the right time. Perhaps even sit and meditate and ask for your sacred space to reveal itself as well as the objects that you should place in it.

It isn't until you come to a spiritual understanding of who you are - not necessarily a religious feeling, but deep down, the spirit within - that you can begin to take control.

~ Oprah Winfrey

Self-Guided Spirit Session:

Have you been anywhere or had a moment when you recognized sacred space? What were some of the qualities of that moment/experience?

_____

_____

_____

_____

_____

_____

_____

_____

_____

_____

_____

_____

_____

_____

_____

_____

_____

_____

_____

Take some of the qualities you listed above about sacred space and pick one or two of them that you can recreate in your own sacred space. Write about the possibilities, and/or if you could notice a difference in implementing these changes.

_____

_____

_____

_____

_____

_____

_____

_____

_____

_____

_____

_____

_____

_____

_____

_____

_____

_____

_____

_____

YOU
DESERVE
TO
RECEIVE

Chapter #9

Unlearning What we Know

One of the most challenging tasks I have ever had has been the act of unlearning many things I have been taught. I had to let go of other people's fear, because it was fueling the flames of my own. I had to unlearn the "truths" of my parents, loved ones, and teachers because they were teaching me everything they believed was right and true for them. I do not fault them because most of it came from love, yet their own filters and perceptions infused their teachings and lessons. I learned how to absorb pain, suffering, and sadness from others who were not capable or willing to feel it for themselves. I learned that my voice was not allowed, my thoughts and actions not acceptable, and most of all I learned it was wrong to be selfish. All of these things were opportunities for me to grow and find my own truths. If you receive nothing else from this book but this one ability, it would be to question everything. Ask yourself why you believe what you believe, and where did it come from? Does it hold true for you or was it once someone else's truth?

Today our world is changing, children are teaching us that our methods of schooling no longer apply. Woman are now the main "bread winners" in their households. Doctors and scientists are proving what the ancients have been trying to tell us for centuries—we are all connected and can heal our lives. Challenge all you have been taught, take what serves you and leave the rest behind. Remember, most people are coming from a loving place when they are sharing their feedback and advice, although this does not mean it applies to you. You can be polite and listen, and not feel obligated to make their way yours.

When I decided to quit my job and pursue my passions, I was very specific about who I shared my plans with. I knew who could support me and who would be projecting their own fear and worry on me. In the back of my mind I could hear them asking, "What if it doesn't work?", "What about your 401K and all of those benefits?", "What about insurance?", "How will you this, and that, etc..". I've learned over time that when I share a dream or a goal I am already going to be experiencing my own self-doubt. I need love and guidance, not criticism and more fear. Some people are very grounded in who they are and can decipher if it is solid advice they are giving or if they are passing along their own misconceptions. Find your tribe of support, people who inspire you and can lift you up and be real with you.

{Spiritual Nudge Wisdom Bit} Practice giving yourself some space and time to decide if something resonates with you or not when having a conversation with someone. Sometimes patterns of self-sabotage or people-pleasing can cause us to immediately commit to an idea, appointment, or belief without first sitting with how it feels to us. Take time, give yourself space, then decide.

Take time to write down your thoughts or responses here:

_____

_____

_____

_____

_____

_____

_____

_____

_____

_____

_____

_____

_____

_____

_____

_____

_____

_____

_____

_____

_____

_____

_____

_____

_____
_____
_____
_____
_____
_____
_____
_____
_____
_____
_____
_____
_____
_____
_____
_____
_____
_____
_____
_____
_____
_____
_____
_____
_____
_____

_The greatest pleasure in life is doing what
people say you cannot do._

~ Walter Bagehot

This all applies to listening to the nudges to your own soul. If you are filling your time and space with the noise of the outside world and everyone else's thoughts, how can you hear your own? More importantly, what are you going to do when the guidance you are receiving internally goes against what someone is telling you, especially when you respect and love them? Having a strong belief and confidence in your own being will help you connect and trust on a more intimate level. I have had many mentors and continue to learn and experience a variety of teachings. Over the years I have had some teachers who taught me what I would never do with my students, and conversely, the best things I could do for my students. Years ago, when I was first recognizing my own spiritual gifts, I ended up with a teacher who taught me the hard way that teachers are still human. He would talk about wonderful spiritual concepts, yet he was operating from ego and ended up having some very shady and unethical experiences that left people angry, frustrated, and with a little less money in their pockets. I am so grateful that I felt that something was out of alignment and left the classes and group before matters got worse.

Our teachers are around us in every moment. My teachers have been young and old, here in physical form and crossed over into spirit. They do not always assume the role of a traditional teacher, sometimes they are a clerk at the grocery store, a child talking back, or a homeless person on the street. Never underestimate spirit to put people in front of you in all forms; never judge a book by its cover. Every moment there is something or someone that can teach you what you need for expansion and growth, if you are open to recognize it for what it is. Even the most difficult of situations has a gift waiting to reveal itself to you.

Self-Guided Spirit Session:

Take a personal inventory. What are three to five qualities/ behaviors that you would like to shift out of?

_____

_____

_____

_____

_____

_____

_____

_____

_____

_____

_____

_____

_____

_____

_____

_____

_____

_____

_____

_____

_____

_____

What is one step you can take action on today to begin the transformation from this quality or behavior?

_____

_____

_____

_____

_____

_____

_____

_____

_____

_____

_____

_____

_____

_____

_____

Never underestimate the power of dreams and the influence of the human spirit. We are all the same in this notion: The potential for greatness lives within each of us.

~ Wilma Rudolph

EXPECT THINGS TO GO YOUR WAY

Chapter #10

Trusting in Yourself First

Learning the language of my soul was not easy for me; I had opportunities to avoid painful situations, if I could have listened. Heartache, trauma, and stress were necessary for me to open my heart and my eyes. Guidance could've allowed me to bypass some of it, but my stubborn nature and immaturity blocked it. There were times when life almost escaped me, and in my need to numb pain, my ego and fears convinced me to shut down the sweet voice of my spirit. When this happened, the learning opportunities continued, repeating patterns and cycles until I understood the lesson or message. Sometimes the message was loud and clear, and was only able to come to light when loss was involved. I lost loved ones to suicide, an extremely painful way for me to learn to love life. Suffering is optional...and so is listening.

Learning to trust in yourself opens the doors to your trusting in your abilities, and cultivating them further. Practice uncovers more understanding of how and why you react the way you do. Becoming a witness to your actions and reactions allows you to step back from the experience. This also reveal the level of emotional attachment and engagement you have within the situation. Emotions are wonderful barometers for attachment. If you have an emotional response, it is guaranteed you have an opportunity for growth within the experience. As you become more confident and gentle with yourself on this journey, there will be a recognition that fear never leaves your life experience, although it can diminish. Fear of change and fear of the unknown are prevalent concerns, so much so that they can keep you from reaching your potential or taking small risks. Some of us are more frightened by the thought of things staying the same. Imagining life not moving forward or changing can create more fear than leaping into the unknown ... it is all a matter of perspective and expectation.

Thinking we know what will happen, then rehashing the details within the mind, opens the door for us to create from that place of fear and dread. The unknown does not have to be scary; quite frankly, it holds all of the potential necessary for you to manifest your dreams. Our perceptions are what we believe, and the energy we feed them through our thoughts and attitudes about life experiences. You can change your perception in any given moment, when you learn how to discipline your thoughts and see the potential of a different outcome. Over time I have learned to love the unknown, because I have a core belief that the unknown is also untapped potential. The more I focus on this idea, the more the universe is able to provide me with evidence that this idea is now becoming my reality. Changing your thoughts will alter your life.

{Spiritual Nudge Wisdom Bit} Take out a pen and piece of paper. Write out five issues or concerns you have had in the past five years. Take each one and write a paragraph about how the issue was resolved, or how a solution came about. Can you notice a pattern or connection between them? Is there a thread of spirit weaved through the experiences?

Take time to write down some of your thoughts or responses here:

_____

_____

_____

_____

_____

_____

_____

_____

_____

_____

_____

_____

_____

_____

_____

_____

_____

_____

_____

_____

_____

_____

_____

_____
_____
_____
_____
_____
_____
_____
_____
_____
_____
_____
_____
_____
_____
_____
_____
_____
_____
_____
_____
_____

Take risks: If you win, you will be happy; if you lose, you will be wise.

~ Anonymous

Trust is a tricky word for most of us; it can bring to mind times when we felt betrayal, hurt, or disappointment. Trust involves letting go, surrendering, and believing it can all work out in your favor. Some of us have been taught we can only trust others when they have first given us reason to believe them and have earned our trust. We're teaching ourselves to only trust when things feel solid and secure, when people prove to us that they are trustworthy.

The universe does not operate in this way. It takes us trusting and believing in something in order for evidence to reveal itself. This is an area where many of us operate from our old limiting beliefs. At some point in our lives we have disappointed ourselves, and most certainly disappointed others. And even though we are human and living on this planet to make mistakes, the accountability we hold towards ourselves on a subconscious level can keep us from living life fully. It is important that we regain our own trust to move forward and to truly live a divine life.

Once we believe in ourselves, we can risk curiosity, wonder, spontaneous delight, or any experience that reveals the human spirit.

~ E. E. cummings

Self-Guided Spirit Session:

Do you truly trust yourself? If so, please explain why. If not, please explain why.

_____

_____

_____

_____

_____

_____

_____

_____

_____

_____

_____

_____

_____

_____

_____

_____

_____

_____

What is one limiting belief about "who you are" that you are
ready to let go of or transform?

_____

_____

_____

_____

_____

_____

_____

_____

_____

_____

_____

_____

_____

_____

_____

_____

_____

_____

_____

_____

_____

RAISE YOURSELF UP WITH JOY

Chapter #11

Taking Action

One of the most crucial pieces to manifestation and listening to your spirit is taking action based upon the guidance you receive. Taking action can generate fear and stop people dead in their tracks, tripping them up. If you have created a stable foundation of trust in yourself, action can feel more natural and fluid. The more you trust yourself, the more you trust your guidance, and the more you can actually put things into action.

Guidance is not always going to make sense; in fact, there will be many times when you may not receive validation until after a situation takes place, when you've already missed the chance to take the action. Your level of stubbornness, and how much you trust yourself will determine the level of comfort you experience and proceed with when moving forward. Sometimes taking action is going to mean speaking up and standing up even when you know you are going to be the only one. Take action with your intuition and walk your talk. How often have you heard someone else say, or maybe it was you, "I knew there was something wrong with that person or that situation, it had all the red flags and I just didn't listen." Now you can fill in the blanks, with anybody, anything, or anyplace. Every one of us is born with the gift of intuition, yet not everyone has the courage to act upon the guidance or the desire to strengthen their innate gifts.

One way to start building confidence when taking action Is asking your spirit for clarity. It is okay to not be 100% certain on the next direction or step to take; this is your opportunity to connect on a deeper level with your spirit. If you do not know the answer, ask for wisdom. Make sure you're not repeating yourself and asking because you are not happy with the answer you're receiving. Our spiritual guidance does not come from a place of ego, and therefore sometimes the messages can seem very simple and not make sense at all. It is helpful to try not to make sense of it, and instead open up and trust in your spirit to guide you. Sometimes you will receive validation on what you are receiving, other times you may never know. The question to ask yourself is, will you still listen to the guidance even if it doesn't make sense?

{Spiritual Nudge Wisdom Bit} Next time you have a situation in which you are feeling blocked in receiving guidance or an answer, take five minutes and go for a walk in nature. If you live in a city area, you can still get some fresh air, and create movement in the body by taking a short stroll. Many times this simple act will clear your head so spirit can reach you.

Take time to write down your thoughts or responses here:

_____
_____
_____
_____
_____
_____
_____
_____
_____
_____
_____
_____
_____
_____
_____
_____
_____
_____
_____
_____
_____
_____
_____
_____
_____
_____

Take a moment now to think about times in your life when you received guidance, and didn't act upon it. Do not harbor regret; remember, you are learning, yet do be aware that it has happened. Make a conscious choice to go forward being more open to receiving the guidance and then creating steps to implement the lessons it gives. It is understandable that you may not want to make a change because you are receiving guidance for a situation, a person, or an experience that isn't healthy for you, yet ask for the next step to take. Do not get lost in the big picture, allow yourself to just to go forward. This idea will help alleviate some of the stress, reduce the overwhelming fear, and give you more opportunities for spirit to reveal support.

Never be in a hurry; do everything quietly and in a calm spirit. Do not lose your inner peace for anything whatsoever, even if your whole world seems upset.

~ Saint Francis de Sales

Visualization for taking action:

1. Write out an example of an issue you are concerned about right now. Close your eyes, take a deep breath, and exhale any tension. Imagine you are breathing in peace, and releasing all the burdens of the mind.

2. Imagine now you're sitting in a beautiful sacred space. Feel relaxed, and open to receive. Ask your spirit to send you a message. With your focus on your breath, continue to breathe in and out slowly and mindfully.

3. As you continue to breathe deeply, notice if you feel lighter or at peace. Allow your spirit to reach you, whether you can see it, feel it, hear it, or sense it. Breathe this energy in for a few more moments.

4. If you have received a message, say thank you; if you haven't received a message, know there is one waiting for you, so open up and receive it; it will come to you in perfect time.

5. Ask your spirit to continue to try and reach you with a message for your highest good, specifically on your next step of action.

Take time to write down your thoughts or responses here:

_____

_____

_____

_____

_____

_____

_____

_____

_____

_____

_____

_____

_____

_____

_____

_____

_____

_____

_____

_____

_____

_____

_____

Self-Guided Spirit Session:

What are five actions steps you are now willing to take?

_____

_____

_____

_____

_____

_____

_____

_____

_____

_____

_____

_____

_____

_____

_____

_____

_____

_____

_____

_____

_____

_____

_____

What are five ways you are going to be held accountable or ask for help with in sticking with these actions?

_____

_____

_____

_____

_____

_____

_____

_____

_____

_____

_____

_____

_____

_____

_____

_____

_____

_____

_____

_____

_____

YOU DO NOT NEED PERMISSION

Chapter #12

Releasing Fear

Fear can be your greatest motivator or your worst enemy, it all depends on how you view it. It is okay to feel hesitant or nervous about connecting with your spirit, just know you will not receive anything you aren't ready to hear or experience. Guidance will never be frightening, it does not contain any ego, and it is for your highest good. Allowing yourself to release the fear and connecting with your spirit can be done very easily so you feel safe and supported. Oftentimes people begin to open up to their intuition and the nudges to their spirit and recognize it's been there all along and there's nothing to fear.

We've all heard this voice inside of us, calling us forward to expand and become a fuller version of ourselves, yet we fear our power. Nudges from your spirit are simply that...gentle nudges. They're kind, they are loving, empowering, supportive, and guiding you through this world. The fear comes from our perception of the guidance. Think of your spirit as a messenger. I like to visualize the owls from the Harry Potter movies (I have wanted one for many years). The owl is simply the messenger, carrying its wisdom to the recipients. The owl didn't write the message, yet is responsible for delivering the information. Your senses are very similar to the owl and spirit is the messenger. If the owl were to interfere with the message, then it's possible it may not be clear or properly delivered. This is very similar to the message of your spirit, when you start to interpret the message or filter it through your senses, it can get muddied and unclear.

It takes discipline and understanding to begin to decipher the message. Be patient and kind with yourself, it is a learning process. There is a beautiful harmony that can exist between your spirit and yourself. Just like learning to ride a bicycle or any new skill, there's a learning curve. For one person that may be falling down a few times, and for someone else it could be recognizing they need a little more practice. It can take a lifetime to truly understand the depth of your spirit. When I was first learning to listen to my messages, one of the most valuable tools I was ever given was instruction on creating an intuition journal. Every day I would write down inspired thoughts, actions, and insights. I would practice listening to the voice of my spirit, and the more attention I placed upon practicing, the more my spirit was revealed to me. Some days the messages were amazing and very clear and other days I felt like I was making it up, like it was all in my head.

{Spiritual Nudge Wisdom Bit} You can create your own intuition journal simply by having a notepad or notebook you dedicate towards these insights. Every time you write in this journal, you're sending a signal to the universe that you are ready to expand. Your spirit will then give you more insight and evidence along your Journey; there is nothing for you to do or try to force to happen, allow it to gently unfold and in its own time.

Take time to write down your thoughts or responses here:

_____

_____

_____

_____

_____

_____

_____

_____

_____

_____

_____

_____

_____

_____

_____

_____

_____

_____

_____

_____

_____

_____

_____

_____

_____

_____

_____

_____

_____

_____

_____

_____

_____

_____

_____

_____

_____

_____

_____

_____

_____

You've got to follow your passion. You've got to figure out what it is you love, who you really are. And have the courage to do that. I believe that the only courage anybody ever needs is the courage to follow your own dreams.

~ Oprah Winfrey

Everything exists in divine timing, and you will never receive any more guidance or information before you are ready to on a soul level. Please note your conscious mind may have a very different opinion as to what you are ready to handle. An intuition journal helps build confidence and allows us to recognize the amount of support you have access to always. In a short amount of time you'll recognize how often you actually do receive messages, and that they were always there; now you are simply just opening your eyes to see them.

As you build this trust in yourself, fear naturally begins to subside and drop away. Then each time you do experience fear, it will change form, intensity, and lessen its hold on you. I like to keep in mind that life experiences, including fear and worry, are indicators that a larger part of my spirit is calling me to expand and grow; therefore, moving through the fear is the antidote that transforms it.

All life is a manifestation of the spirit, the manifestation of love.

~ Morihei Ueshiba

Self-Guided Spirit Session:

Are your fears rational or irrational? A helpful way to determine this is whether they have a "story" attached to them. A fear of something without a prior experience, connection, or obvious threat could likely be an irrational fear.

_____

_____

_____

_____

_____

_____

_____

_____

_____

_____

_____

_____

_____

_____

_____

_____

_____

What are some fears you are ready to explore and release?

_____

_____

_____

_____

_____

_____

_____

_____

_____

_____

_____

_____

_____

_____

_____

_____

_____

_____

_____

_____

_____

_____

_____

YOU
ARE
GOOD
ENOUGH

A Special Message to You

A beautiful message from spirit to you:

Sweet child of God, you are so very loved. If you only knew the wealth of love and support you have on this journey, you would never again feel fear. You would walk this divine path knowing you are held in love and light, and through our eyes we see you as nothing less than love. The potential within you and around you is always there, allow you to release your limitations so that you may see yourself the way we see you.

There is nothing for you to do or achieve, simply allow us to comfort you and walk with you along this journey. Lean on us when you are questioning everything, talk to us when you need to know you are not alone, call on us when you're feeling any less then loving within that beautiful heart of yours. We're always here and always have been here to guide you forward; you have unlimited potential. Release the past, it is safe for you to be in the present moment, and this frees you up from fearing the future. There is no future, it is right now, and you have all the power of the universe behind you to back you up, to guide you, to support you, to lead you, to direct you, to teach you, and to instruct you; do not feel fear, my dear child. Forgive yourself and forgive others as we all are teachers and students in this giant classroom of life, and if you could only see the gifts given to you from fear and painful experiences you would forever understand the beauty of the lesson. It was never to punish you, only to help your expansion. You have a wonderful place on this earth at this time, do not allow your attention to go towards questioning your purpose, only allow your attention to go to what feels in alignment for you and to all of your actions, thoughts, and deeds.

I know what it feels like to stay in the shadows and hide; I lived in that place for many years and it still finds its way into my life when I veer off my path. I have learned that it is safe to be seen and not only is it safe, it is necessary. There are people in this world that need you to show up. Trust in that, it is what your spirit has been calling you towards.

Blessings always & in all ways

~Melissa

The Intuition Journal

NUDGES FROM YOUR SPIRIT

Nudges from Your Spirit Intuition Journal

This journal was created to remind you of the whisper of spirit in every moment of your life. When we bring attention to support, guidance, and messages, they increase and multiply. Utilize the journal and get into a practice of noticing the messages, it will become more comfortable and the mental chatter will subside.

Every day you choose to witness the blessings and gifts from spirit, the heavens rejoice with love and excitement and ancestors and guides come forward at the first call to assist.

The Rules

There are none, aside from allowing your thoughts and ideas to flow. Do not get into your head trying to question if something was spirit or a "coincidence"; allow the magic of the experience to be enough for you to begin trusting in the process. Refrain from censoring, editing, or judging the words, experiences, or awareness that you write in your journal.

The Journal Prompts

The prompts are simply ideas for you to ponder in order to open your heart and mind. You may follow them or go with the nudge of your own spirit to write about what you are feeling called to understand.

There is one prompt for the date and how you were aware of spirit's presence for that date. This is a place where you can write about specific things that occurred throughout your day. The second prompt is to acknowledge how you felt during and after the experiences of the day. This section is to help you discover your mental and emotional state as you receive guidance and how you might process that information. The third prompt is to help you discover if there are action steps needed with the guidance, or simply new ideas and beliefs that are becoming part of your con- sciousness.

{Day 1 of 44} Today's Date:

Today I was aware of spirits' presence when I observed or witnessed:

_____

_____

_____

_____

_____

_____

_____

_____

_____

_____

_____

_____

_____

_____

_____

_____

_____

_____

_____

_____

_____

_____

_____

Today I noticed how I was feeling about the presence of spirit, or my experiences today:

_____

_____

_____

_____

_____

_____

_____

_____

_____

_____

_____

_____

_____

_____

_____

_____

_____

_____

_____

_____

_____

_____

_____

_____

Possible actions steps, additional nudges and forward motion
I can take or acknowledge:

_____

_____

_____

_____

_____

_____

_____

_____

_____

_____

_____

_____

_____

_____

_____

_____

_____

_____

_____

_____

_____

_____

{Day 2 of 44} Today's Date:

Today I was aware of spirits' presence when I observed or witnessed:

_____

_____

_____

_____

_____

_____

_____

_____

_____

_____

_____

_____

_____

_____

_____

_____

_____

_____

_____

_____

_____

_____

Today I noticed how I was feeling about the presence of spirit, or my experiences today:

_____

_____

_____

_____

_____

_____

_____

_____

_____

_____

_____

_____

_____

_____

_____

_____

_____

_____

_____

_____

_____

_____

_____

_____

Possible actions steps, additional nudges and forward motion
I can take or acknowledge:

_____

_____

_____

_____

_____

_____

_____

_____

_____

_____

_____

_____

_____

_____

_____

_____

_____

_____

_____

_____

_____

{Day 3 of 44} Today's Date:

Today I was aware of spirits' presence when I observed or witnessed:

_____

_____

_____

_____

_____

_____

_____

_____

_____

_____

_____

_____

_____

_____

_____

_____

_____

_____

_____

_____

Today I noticed how I was feeling about the presence of spirit, or my experiences today:

_____

_____

_____

_____

_____

_____

_____

_____

_____

_____

_____

_____

_____

_____

_____

_____

_____

_____

_____

_____

_____

_____

Possible actions steps, additional nudges and forward motion
I can take or acknowledge:

_____

_____

_____

_____

_____

_____

_____

_____

_____

_____

_____

_____

_____

_____

_____

_____

_____

_____

_____

_____

_____

_____

{Day 4 of 44} Today's Date:

Today I was aware of spirits' presence when I observed or witnessed:

_____

_____

_____

_____

_____

_____

_____

_____

_____

_____

_____

_____

_____

_____

_____

_____

_____

_____

_____

_____

Today I noticed how I was feeling about the presence of spirit, or my experiences today:

_____

_____

_____

_____

_____

_____

_____

_____

_____

_____

_____

_____

_____

_____

_____

_____

_____

_____

_____

_____

_____

_____

Possible actions steps, additional nudges and forward motion
I can take or acknowledge:

_____

_____

_____

_____

_____

_____

_____

_____

_____

_____

_____

_____

_____

_____

_____

_____

_____

_____

_____

_____

{Day 5 of 44} Today's Date:

Today I was aware of spirits' presence when I observed or witnessed:

_____

_____

_____

_____

_____

_____

_____

_____

_____

_____

_____

_____

_____

_____

_____

_____

_____

_____

_____

_____

_____

Today I noticed how I was feeling about the presence of spirit, or my experiences today:

_____

_____

_____

_____

_____

_____

_____

_____

_____

_____

_____

_____

_____

_____

_____

_____

_____

_____

_____

_____

_____

_____

_____

Possible actions steps, additional nudges and forward motion
I can take or acknowledge:

_____

_____

_____

_____

_____

_____

_____

_____

_____

_____

_____

_____

_____

_____

_____

_____

_____

_____

_____

_____

_____

{Day 6 of 44} Today's Date:

Today I was aware of spirits' presence when I observed or witnessed:

_____

_____

_____

_____

_____

_____

_____

_____

_____

_____

_____

_____

_____

_____

_____

_____

_____

_____

_____

Today I noticed how I was feeling about the presence of spirit, or my experiences today:

_____

_____

_____

_____

_____

_____

_____

_____

_____

_____

_____

_____

_____

_____

_____

_____

_____

_____

_____

_____

_____

_____

Possible actions steps, additional nudges and forward motion
I can take or acknowledge:

_____

_____

_____

_____

_____

_____

_____

_____

_____

_____

_____

_____

_____

_____

_____

_____

_____

_____

_____

_____

_____

_____

{Day 7 of 44} Today's Date:

Today I was aware of spirits' presence when I observed or witnessed:

_____

_____

_____

_____

_____

_____

_____

_____

_____

_____

_____

_____

_____

_____

_____

_____

_____

_____

_____

_____

Today I noticed how I was feeling about the presence of spirit, or my experiences today:

_____

_____

_____

_____

_____

_____

_____

_____

_____

_____

_____

_____

_____

_____

_____

_____

_____

_____

_____

_____

_____

_____

_____

Possible actions steps, additional nudges and forward motion
I can take or acknowledge:

_____

_____

_____

_____

_____

_____

_____

_____

_____

_____

_____

_____

_____

_____

_____

_____

_____

_____

_____

_____

_____

_____

{Day 8 of 44} Today's Date:

Today I was aware of spirits' presence when I observed or witnessed:

_____

_____

_____

_____

_____

_____

_____

_____

_____

_____

_____

_____

_____

_____

_____

_____

_____

_____

_____

Today I noticed how I was feeling about the presence of spirit, or my experiences today:

_____

_____

_____

_____

_____

_____

_____

_____

_____

_____

_____

_____

_____

_____

_____

_____

_____

_____

_____

_____

_____

_____

Possible actions steps, additional nudges and forward motion I can take or acknowledge:

_____

_____

_____

_____

_____

_____

_____

_____

_____

_____

_____

_____

_____

_____

_____

_____

_____

_____

_____

_____

{Day 9 of 44} Today's Date:

Today I was aware of spirits' presence when I observed or witnessed:

_____

_____

_____

_____

_____

_____

_____

_____

_____

_____

_____

_____

_____

_____

_____

_____

_____

_____

_____

_____

_____

_____

Today I noticed how I was feeling about the presence of spirit, or my experiences today:

_____

_____

_____

_____

_____

_____

_____

_____

_____

_____

_____

_____

_____

_____

_____

_____

_____

_____

_____

_____

_____

_____

_____

Possible actions steps, additional nudges and forward motion
I can take or acknowledge:

_____

_____

_____

_____

_____

_____

_____

_____

_____

_____

_____

_____

_____

_____

_____

_____

_____

_____

_____

_____

_____

{Day 10 of 44} Today's Date:

Today I was aware of spirits' presence when I observed or witnessed:

_____

_____

_____

_____

_____

_____

_____

_____

_____

_____

_____

_____

_____

_____

_____

_____

_____

_____

_____

Today I noticed how I was feeling about the presence of spirit, or my experiences today:

_____

_____

_____

_____

_____

_____

_____

_____

_____

_____

_____

_____

_____

_____

_____

_____

_____

_____

_____

_____

_____

_____

_____

Possible actions steps, additional nudges and forward motion
I can take or acknowledge:

_____

_____

_____

_____

_____

_____

_____

_____

_____

_____

_____

_____

_____

_____

_____

_____

_____

_____

_____

_____

_____

_____

{Day 11 of 44} Today's Date:

Today I was aware of spirits' presence when I observed or
witnessed:

_____

_____

_____

_____

_____

_____

_____

_____

_____

_____

_____

_____

_____

_____

_____

_____

_____

_____

_____

_____

_____

_____

Today I noticed how I was feeling about the presence of spirit, or my experiences today:

_____

_____

_____

_____

_____

_____

_____

_____

_____

_____

_____

_____

_____

_____

_____

_____

_____

_____

_____

_____

_____

_____

Possible actions steps, additional nudges and forward motion
I can take or acknowledge:

_____

_____

_____

_____

_____

_____

_____

_____

_____

_____

_____

_____

_____

_____

_____

_____

_____

_____

_____

_____

{Day 12 of 44} Today's Date:

Today I was aware of spirits' presence when I observed or witnessed:

_____

_____

_____

_____

_____

_____

_____

_____

_____

_____

_____

_____

_____

_____

_____

_____

_____

_____

_____

Today I noticed how I was feeling about the presence of spirit, or my experiences today:

_____

_____

_____

_____

_____

_____

_____

_____

_____

_____

_____

_____

_____

_____

_____

_____

_____

_____

_____

_____

_____

_____

_____

_____

Possible actions steps, additional nudges and forward motion
I can take or acknowledge:

_____

_____

_____

_____

_____

_____

_____

_____

_____

_____

_____

_____

_____

_____

_____

_____

_____

_____

_____

_____

_____

{Day 13 of 44} Today's Date:

Today I was aware of spirits' presence when I observed or witnessed:

_____

_____

_____

_____

_____

_____

_____

_____

_____

_____

_____

_____

_____

_____

_____

_____

_____

_____

_____

_____

Today I noticed how I was feeling about the presence of spirit, or my experiences today:

_____

_____

_____

_____

_____

_____

_____

_____

_____

_____

_____

_____

_____

_____

_____

_____

_____

_____

_____

_____

_____

_____

_____

Possible actions steps, additional nudges and forward motion
I can take or acknowledge:

_____

_____

_____

_____

_____

_____

_____

_____

_____

_____

_____

_____

_____

_____

_____

_____

_____

_____

_____

_____

_____

{Day 14 of 44} Today's Date:

Today I was aware of spirits' presence when I observed or witnessed:

_____

_____

_____

_____

_____

_____

_____

_____

_____

_____

_____

_____

_____

_____

_____

_____

_____

_____

_____

Today I noticed how I was feeling about the presence of spirit, or my experiences today:

_____

_____

_____

_____

_____

_____

_____

_____

_____

_____

_____

_____

_____

_____

_____

_____

_____

_____

_____

_____

_____

Possible actions steps, additional nudges and forward motion
I can take or acknowledge:

_____

_____

_____

_____

_____

_____

_____

_____

_____

_____

_____

_____

_____

_____

_____

_____

_____

_____

_____

_____

{Day 15 of 44} Today's Date:

Today I was aware of spirits' presence when I observed or witnessed:

_____

_____

_____

_____

_____

_____

_____

_____

_____

_____

_____

_____

_____

_____

_____

_____

_____

_____

_____

Today I noticed how I was feeling about the presence of spirit, or my experiences today:

_____

_____

_____

_____

_____

_____

_____

_____

_____

_____

_____

_____

_____

_____

_____

_____

_____

_____

_____

_____

_____

_____

_____

_____

Possible actions steps, additional nudges and forward motion
I can take or acknowledge:

_____

_____

_____

_____

_____

_____

_____

_____

_____

_____

_____

_____

_____

_____

_____

_____

_____

_____

_____

_____

{Day 16 of 44} Today's Date:

Today I was aware of spirits' presence when I observed or witnessed:

_____

_____

_____

_____

_____

_____

_____

_____

_____

_____

_____

_____

_____

_____

_____

_____

_____

_____

_____

Today I noticed how I was feeling about the presence of spirit, or my experiences today:

_____

_____

_____

_____

_____

_____

_____

_____

_____

_____

_____

_____

_____

_____

_____

_____

_____

_____

_____

_____

_____

_____

Possible actions steps, additional nudges and forward motion
I can take or acknowledge:

_____

_____

_____

_____

_____

_____

_____

_____

_____

_____

_____

_____

_____

_____

_____

_____

_____

_____

_____

_____

_____

{Day 17 of 44} Today's Date:

Today I was aware of spirits' presence when I observed or witnessed:

_____

_____

_____

_____

_____

_____

_____

_____

_____

_____

_____

_____

_____

_____

_____

_____

_____

_____

_____

_____

_____

Today I noticed how I was feeling about the presence of spirit, or my experiences today:

_____

_____

_____

_____

_____

_____

_____

_____

_____

_____

_____

_____

_____

_____

_____

_____

_____

_____

_____

_____

_____

_____

Possible actions steps, additional nudges and forward motion
I can take or acknowledge:

_____

_____

_____

_____

_____

_____

_____

_____

_____

_____

_____

_____

_____

_____

_____

_____

_____

_____

_____

_____

{Day 18 of 44} Today's Date:

Today I was aware of spirits' presence when I observed or witnessed:

_____

_____

_____

_____

_____

_____

_____

_____

_____

_____

_____

_____

_____

_____

_____

_____

_____

_____

_____

_____

Today I noticed how I was feeling about the presence of spirit, or my experiences today:

_____

_____

_____

_____

_____

_____

_____

_____

_____

_____

_____

_____

_____

_____

_____

_____

_____

_____

_____

_____

_____

Possible actions steps, additional nudges and forward motion
I can take or acknowledge:

_____

_____

_____

_____

_____

_____

_____

_____

_____

_____

_____

_____

_____

_____

_____

_____

_____

_____

_____

_____

_____

_____

{Day 19 of 44} Today's Date:

Today I was aware of spirits' presence when I observed or witnessed:

_____

_____

_____

_____

_____

_____

_____

_____

_____

_____

_____

_____

_____

_____

_____

_____

_____

_____

_____

_____

_____

_____

Today I noticed how I was feeling about the presence of spirit, or my experiences today:

_____

_____

_____

_____

_____

_____

_____

_____

_____

_____

_____

_____

_____

_____

_____

_____

_____

_____

_____

_____

_____

_____

Possible actions steps, additional nudges and forward motion
I can take or acknowledge:

_____

_____

_____

_____

_____

_____

_____

_____

_____

_____

_____

_____

_____

_____

_____

_____

_____

_____

_____

_____

_____

_____

{Day 20 of 44} Today's Date:

Today I was aware of spirits' presence when I observed or witnessed:

_____

_____

_____

_____

_____

_____

_____

_____

_____

_____

_____

_____

_____

_____

_____

_____

_____

_____

_____

_____

Today I noticed how I was feeling about the presence of spirit, or my experiences today:

_____

_____

_____

_____

_____

_____

_____

_____

_____

_____

_____

_____

_____

_____

_____

_____

_____

_____

_____

_____

_____

_____

_____

Possible actions steps, additional nudges and forward motion
I can take or acknowledge:

_____

_____

_____

_____

_____

_____

_____

_____

_____

_____

_____

_____

_____

_____

_____

_____

_____

_____

_____

_____

_____

{Day 21 of 44} Today's Date:

Today I was aware of spirits' presence when I observed or witnessed:

_____

_____

_____

_____

_____

_____

_____

_____

_____

_____

_____

_____

_____

_____

_____

_____

_____

_____

_____

_____

_____

_____

_____

Today I noticed how I was feeling about the presence of spirit, or my experiences today:

_____

_____

_____

_____

_____

_____

_____

_____

_____

_____

_____

_____

_____

_____

_____

_____

_____

_____

_____

_____

_____

_____

Possible actions steps, additional nudges and forward motion
I can take or acknowledge:

_____

_____

_____

_____

_____

_____

_____

_____

_____

_____

_____

_____

_____

_____

_____

_____

_____

_____

_____

_____

{Day 22 of 44} Today's Date:

Today I was aware of spirits' presence when I observed or witnessed:

_____

_____

_____

_____

_____

_____

_____

_____

_____

_____

_____

_____

_____

_____

_____

_____

_____

_____

_____

_____

Today I noticed how I was feeling about the presence of spirit, or my experiences today:

_____

_____

_____

_____

_____

_____

_____

_____

_____

_____

_____

_____

_____

_____

_____

_____

_____

_____

_____

_____

_____

_____

Possible actions steps, additional nudges and forward motion
I can take or acknowledge:

_____

_____

_____

_____

_____

_____

_____

_____

_____

_____

_____

_____

_____

_____

_____

_____

_____

_____

_____

_____

{Day 23 of 44} Today's Date:

Today I was aware of spirits' presence when I observed or witnessed:

_____

_____

_____

_____

_____

_____

_____

_____

_____

_____

_____

_____

_____

_____

_____

_____

_____

_____

_____

_____

_____

_____

Today I noticed how I was feeling about the presence of spirit, or my experiences today:

_____

_____

_____

_____

_____

_____

_____

_____

_____

_____

_____

_____

_____

_____

_____

_____

_____

_____

_____

_____

_____

_____

_____

_____

Possible actions steps, additional nudges and forward motion
I can take or acknowledge:

_____

_____

_____

_____

_____

_____

_____

_____

_____

_____

_____

_____

_____

_____

_____

_____

_____

_____

_____

_____

_____

{Day 24 of 44} Today's Date:

Today I was aware of spirits' presence when I observed or witnessed:

_____

_____

_____

_____

_____

_____

_____

_____

_____

_____

_____

_____

_____

_____

_____

_____

_____

_____

_____

_____

_____

_____

Today I noticed how I was feeling about the presence of spirit, or my experiences today:

_____

_____

_____

_____

_____

_____

_____

_____

_____

_____

_____

_____

_____

_____

_____

_____

_____

_____

_____

_____

_____

_____

_____

Possible actions steps, additional nudges and forward motion
I can take or acknowledge:

_____

_____

_____

_____

_____

_____

_____

_____

_____

_____

_____

_____

_____

_____

_____

_____

_____

_____

_____

_____

_____

{Day 25 of 44} Today's Date:

Today I was aware of spirits' presence when I observed or witnessed:

_____

_____

_____

_____

_____

_____

_____

_____

_____

_____

_____

_____

_____

_____

_____

_____

_____

_____

_____

_____

_____

_____

_____

Today I noticed how I was feeling about the presence of spirit, or my experiences today:

_____

_____

_____

_____

_____

_____

_____

_____

_____

_____

_____

_____

_____

_____

_____

_____

_____

_____

_____

_____

_____

_____

Possible actions steps, additional nudges and forward motion
I can take or acknowledge:

_____

_____

_____

_____

_____

_____

_____

_____

_____

_____

_____

_____

_____

_____

_____

_____

_____

_____

_____

_____

_____

{Day 26 of 44} Today's Date:

Today I was aware of spirits' presence when I observed or witnessed:

_____

_____

_____

_____

_____

_____

_____

_____

_____

_____

_____

_____

_____

_____

_____

_____

_____

_____

_____

_____

Today I noticed how I was feeling about the presence of spirit, or my experiences today:

_____

_____

_____

_____

_____

_____

_____

_____

_____

_____

_____

_____

_____

_____

_____

_____

_____

_____

_____

_____

_____

_____

_____

Possible actions steps, additional nudges and forward motion
I can take or acknowledge:

_____

_____

_____

_____

_____

_____

_____

_____

_____

_____

_____

_____

_____

_____

_____

_____

_____

_____

_____

_____

{Day 27 of 44} Today's Date:

Today I was aware of spirits' presence when I observed or witnessed:

_____

_____

_____

_____

_____

_____

_____

_____

_____

_____

_____

_____

_____

_____

_____

_____

_____

_____

_____

_____

_____

Today I noticed how I was feeling about the presence of spirit, or my experiences today:

_____

_____

_____

_____

_____

_____

_____

_____

_____

_____

_____

_____

_____

_____

_____

_____

_____

_____

_____

_____

_____

_____

_____

_____

Possible actions steps, additional nudges and forward motion
I can take or acknowledge:

_____

_____

_____

_____

_____

_____

_____

_____

_____

_____

_____

_____

_____

_____

_____

_____

_____

_____

_____

_____

_____

_____

{Day 28 of 44} Today's Date:

Today I was aware of spirits' presence when I observed or witnessed:

_____

_____

_____

_____

_____

_____

_____

_____

_____

_____

_____

_____

_____

_____

_____

_____

_____

_____

_____

_____

Today I noticed how I was feeling about the presence of spirit, or my experiences today:

_____

_____

_____

_____

_____

_____

_____

_____

_____

_____

_____

_____

_____

_____

_____

_____

_____

_____

_____

_____

_____

_____

_____

Possible actions steps, additional nudges and forward motion
I can take or acknowledge:

_____

_____

_____

_____

_____

_____

_____

_____

_____

_____

_____

_____

_____

_____

_____

_____

_____

_____

_____

_____

_____

{Day 29 of 44} Today's Date:

Today I was aware of spirits' presence when I observed or witnessed:

_____

_____

_____

_____

_____

_____

_____

_____

_____

_____

_____

_____

_____

_____

_____

_____

_____

_____

_____

_____

_____

Today I noticed how I was feeling about the presence of spirit, or my experiences today:

_____

_____

_____

_____

_____

_____

_____

_____

_____

_____

_____

_____

_____

_____

_____

_____

_____

_____

_____

_____

_____

_____

Possible actions steps, additional nudges and forward motion I can take or acknowledge:

_____

_____

_____

_____

_____

_____

_____

_____

_____

_____

_____

_____

_____

_____

_____

_____

_____

_____

_____

_____

_____

{Day 30 of 44} Today's Date:

Today I was aware of spirits' presence when I observed or witnessed:

_____

_____

_____

_____

_____

_____

_____

_____

_____

_____

_____

_____

_____

_____

_____

_____

_____

_____

_____

_____

_____

Today I noticed how I was feeling about the presence of spirit, or my experiences today:

_____

_____

_____

_____

_____

_____

_____

_____

_____

_____

_____

_____

_____

_____

_____

_____

_____

_____

_____

_____

_____

Possible actions steps, additional nudges and forward motion
I can take or acknowledge:

_____

_____

_____

_____

_____

_____

_____

_____

_____

_____

_____

_____

_____

_____

_____

_____

_____

_____

_____

_____

_____

{Day 31 of 44} Today's Date:

Today I was aware of spirits' presence when I observed or witnessed:

_____

_____

_____

_____

_____

_____

_____

_____

_____

_____

_____

_____

_____

_____

_____

_____

_____

_____

_____

_____

_____

Today I noticed how I was feeling about the presence of spirit, or my experiences today:

_____

_____

_____

_____

_____

_____

_____

_____

_____

_____

_____

_____

_____

_____

_____

_____

_____

_____

_____

_____

_____

_____

Possible actions steps, additional nudges and forward motion
I can take or acknowledge:

_____

_____

_____

_____

_____

_____

_____

_____

_____

_____

_____

_____

_____

_____

_____

_____

_____

_____

_____

_____

{Day 32 of 44} Today's Date:

Today I was aware of spirits' presence when I observed or witnessed:

_____

_____

_____

_____

_____

_____

_____

_____

_____

_____

_____

_____

_____

_____

_____

_____

_____

_____

_____

_____

_____

_____

Today I noticed how I was feeling about the presence of spirit, or my experiences today:

_____

_____

_____

_____

_____

_____

_____

_____

_____

_____

_____

_____

_____

_____

_____

_____

_____

_____

_____

_____

_____

_____

_____

Possible actions steps, additional nudges and forward motion I can take or acknowledge:

_____

_____

_____

_____

_____

_____

_____

_____

_____

_____

_____

_____

_____

_____

_____

_____

_____

_____

_____

{Day 33 of 44} Today's Date:

Today I was aware of spirits' presence when I observed or witnessed:

_____

_____

_____

_____

_____

_____

_____

_____

_____

_____

_____

_____

_____

_____

_____

_____

_____

_____

_____

_____

_____

Today I noticed how I was feeling about the presence of spirit, or my experiences today:

_____

_____

_____

_____

_____

_____

_____

_____

_____

_____

_____

_____

_____

_____

_____

_____

_____

_____

_____

_____

_____

_____

_____

_____

Possible actions steps, additional nudges and forward motion
I can take or acknowledge:

_____

_____

_____

_____

_____

_____

_____

_____

_____

_____

_____

_____

_____

_____

_____

_____

_____

_____

_____

_____

_____

_____

{Day 34 of 44} Today's Date:

Today I was aware of spirits' presence when I observed or
witnessed:

_____

_____

_____

_____

_____

_____

_____

_____

_____

_____

_____

_____

_____

_____

_____

_____

_____

_____

_____

_____

Today I noticed how I was feeling about the presence of spirit, or my experiences today:

_____

_____

_____

_____

_____

_____

_____

_____

_____

_____

_____

_____

_____

_____

_____

_____

_____

_____

_____

_____

_____

_____

Possible actions steps, additional nudges and forward motion
I can take or acknowledge:

_____

_____

_____

_____

_____

_____

_____

_____

_____

_____

_____

_____

_____

_____

_____

_____

_____

_____

_____

_____

_____

{Day 35 of 44} Today's Date:

Today I was aware of spirits' presence when I observed or witnessed:

_____

_____

_____

_____

_____

_____

_____

_____

_____

_____

_____

_____

_____

_____

_____

_____

_____

_____

_____

_____

Today I noticed how I was feeling about the presence of spirit, or my experiences today:

_____

_____

_____

_____

_____

_____

_____

_____

_____

_____

_____

_____

_____

_____

_____

_____

_____

_____

_____

_____

_____

_____

_____

Possible actions steps, additional nudges and forward motion
I can take or acknowledge:

_____

_____

_____

_____

_____

_____

_____

_____

_____

_____

_____

_____

_____

_____

_____

_____

_____

_____

_____

_____

_____

{Day 36 of 44} Today's Date:

Today I was aware of spirits' presence when I observed or witnessed:

_____

_____

_____

_____

_____

_____

_____

_____

_____

_____

_____

_____

_____

_____

_____

_____

_____

_____

_____

_____

Today I noticed how I was feeling about the presence of spirit, or my experiences today:

_____

_____

_____

_____

_____

_____

_____

_____

_____

_____

_____

_____

_____

_____

_____

_____

_____

_____

_____

_____

_____

_____

_____

_____

Possible actions steps, additional nudges and forward motion
I can take or acknowledge:

_____

_____

_____

_____

_____

_____

_____

_____

_____

_____

_____

_____

_____

_____

_____

_____

_____

_____

_____

_____

_____

_____

_____

_____

{Day 37 of 44} Today's Date:

Today I was aware of spirits' presence when I observed or witnessed:

_____

_____

_____

_____

_____

_____

_____

_____

_____

_____

_____

_____

_____

_____

_____

_____

_____

_____

_____

_____

_____

_____

Today I noticed how I was feeling about the presence of spirit, or my experiences today:

_____

_____

_____

_____

_____

_____

_____

_____

_____

_____

_____

_____

_____

_____

_____

_____

_____

_____

_____

_____

_____

_____

Possible actions steps, additional nudges and forward motion
I can take or acknowledge:

_____

_____

_____

_____

_____

_____

_____

_____

_____

_____

_____

_____

_____

_____

_____

_____

_____

_____

_____

_____

_____

{Day 38 of 44} Today's Date:

Today I was aware of spirits' presence when I observed or witnessed:

_____

_____

_____

_____

_____

_____

_____

_____

_____

_____

_____

_____

_____

_____

_____

_____

_____

_____

_____

_____

_____

Today I noticed how I was feeling about the presence of spirit, or my experiences today:

_____

_____

_____

_____

_____

_____

_____

_____

_____

_____

_____

_____

_____

_____

_____

_____

_____

_____

_____

_____

Possible actions steps, additional nudges and forward motion
I can take or acknowledge:

_____

_____

_____

_____

_____

_____

_____

_____

_____

_____

_____

_____

_____

_____

_____

_____

_____

_____

_____

_____

_____

_____

{Day 39 of 44} Today's Date:

Today I was aware of spirits' presence when I observed or witnessed:

_____

_____

_____

_____

_____

_____

_____

_____

_____

_____

_____

_____

_____

_____

_____

_____

_____

_____

_____

Today I noticed how I was feeling about the presence of spirit, or my experiences today:

_____

_____

_____

_____

_____

_____

_____

_____

_____

_____

_____

_____

_____

_____

_____

_____

_____

_____

_____

_____

_____

_____

Possible actions steps, additional nudges and forward motion
I can take or acknowledge:

_____

_____

_____

_____

_____

_____

_____

_____

_____

_____

_____

_____

_____

_____

_____

_____

_____

_____

_____

_____

_____

_____

_____

{Day 40 of 44} Today's Date:

Today I was aware of spirits' presence when I observed or witnessed:

_____

_____

_____

_____

_____

_____

_____

_____

_____

_____

_____

_____

_____

_____

_____

_____

_____

_____

_____

_____

_____

Today I noticed how I was feeling about the presence of spirit, or my experiences today:

_____

_____

_____

_____

_____

_____

_____

_____

_____

_____

_____

_____

_____

_____

_____

_____

_____

_____

_____

_____

_____

_____

Possible actions steps, additional nudges and forward motion
I can take or acknowledge:

_____

_____

_____

_____

_____

_____

_____

_____

_____

_____

_____

_____

_____

_____

_____

_____

_____

_____

_____

_____

_____

_____

{Day 41 of 44} Today's Date:

Today I was aware of spirits' presence when I observed or witnessed:

_____

_____

_____

_____

_____

_____

_____

_____

_____

_____

_____

_____

_____

_____

_____

_____

_____

_____

_____

_____

_____

Today I noticed how I was feeling about the presence of spirit, or my experiences today:

_____

_____

_____

_____

_____

_____

_____

_____

_____

_____

_____

_____

_____

_____

_____

_____

_____

_____

_____

_____

_____

_____

_____

_____

Possible actions steps, additional nudges and forward motion
I can take or acknowledge:

_____

_____

_____

_____

_____

_____

_____

_____

_____

_____

_____

_____

_____

_____

_____

_____

_____

_____

_____

_____

_____

{Day 42 of 44} Today's Date:

Today I was aware of spirits' presence when I observed or witnessed:

_____

_____

_____

_____

_____

_____

_____

_____

_____

_____

_____

_____

_____

_____

_____

_____

_____

_____

_____

_____

_____

Today I noticed how I was feeling about the presence of spirit, or my experiences today:

_____

_____

_____

_____

_____

_____

_____

_____

_____

_____

_____

_____

_____

_____

_____

_____

_____

_____

_____

_____

_____

Possible actions steps, additional nudges and forward motion I can take or acknowledge:

_____

_____

_____

_____

_____

_____

_____

_____

_____

_____

_____

_____

_____

_____

_____

_____

_____

_____

_____

_____

_____

{Day 43 of 44} Today's Date:

Today I was aware of spirits' presence when I observed or witnessed:

_____

_____

_____

_____

_____

_____

_____

_____

_____

_____

_____

_____

_____

_____

_____

_____

_____

_____

_____

_____

_____

_____

_____

Today I noticed how I was feeling about the presence of spirit, or my experiences today:

_____

_____

_____

_____

_____

_____

_____

_____

_____

_____

_____

_____

_____

_____

_____

_____

_____

_____

_____

_____

_____

_____

_____

Possible actions steps, additional nudges and forward motion
I can take or acknowledge:

_____

_____

_____

_____

_____

_____

_____

_____

_____

_____

_____

_____

_____

_____

_____

_____

_____

_____

_____

_____

_____

_____

_____

About Melissa Kim Corter

Melissa Kim Corter is a spiritual teacher, author, and soul artist. She has a gift of capturing the essence of her client's, while providing a safe space, and unconditional love to help them release their fears of "being seen" or putting themselves more fully out into the world. Over time Melissa  recognized that each client reflected back to her opportunities for healing, expansion, and discovering the power of their own light. This became the foundation of her company, "Soul Artistry®", a company founded to help women release fear, step into their power, and claim their place in this universe!

As a spiritual teacher Melissa has discovered the power of helping others reclaim the truth of who they are: a divine spiritual being in a body. Her gifts include sacred sight, a method of using her camera as a tool, and guiding women gently to feel safe and to embrace their divinity. As a certified hypnotherapist and yoga teacher, Melissa also discovered the importance of listening to her spirit and "soul tribe" (her team of guides that help her do her work). She teaches others how to tap into the wisdom that their unique spirit is guiding them to find, so they can share their authenticity with the world.

With over 15 years of experience in the mind, body, spirit industry Melissa built a holistic practice of clients and students with her unique style and combination of healing modalities and artistic talent. They started coming to her for a unique blending of services including hypnotherapy, spiritual counseling, soul artistry, and shamanism.

Even though her journey began as a photographer looking for beauty in the world, she discovered that everyone is a reflection of each other; we see in others what we want to see, or are not wanting to see. It then became her intention to see everyone through the eyes and lens of love ... which then unfolded her own journey of learning how to love herself.

Other Products & Services
By Melissa Kim Corter

* All of the following can be found on her website: www.melissacorter.com

Card deck: Nudges From Your Spirit

Weaved throughout this book you may have noticed pages with affirmative statements written on them. These statements are actual messages from the card deck Nudges From Your Spirit. This deck contains 44 powerful messages for helping you connect with your own spirit.

E-Course: Nudges From Your Spirit

Want to explore this book and connect further with your own spirit? You can sign up for the online course at any time. This course is 5 modules long with the course materials available online. It is filled with lessons, examples, stories, and audios for you to listen to. Once you go through it, then it is your to keep and revisit at any time!

Nidra Meditations

Nidra is a form of meditation that Melissa contributes to saving her life. This practice is for anyone who has a restless mind and spirit, cannot slow down their thoughts, and has some emotional healing they wish to support. This style of meditation is transformative and has helped people with anxiety, PTSD, addiction, trauma, depression, fear, stress, anger, and more. It is unlimited in how it can help release patterns from the subconscious mind.

Seasons of Change- Invoking the moon and the magic of the elements Course

This course is is a fun way to learn about the seasons (solstices & equinoxes), the cycles of the moon, and the power of the four elements: earth, water, fire, and air. Each call is recorded and jam packed with information with a private Facebook support group.

Prosperity Intensive: Manifesting with Magic

This course is to shift how you attract & relate to prosperity. Insight and lessons to help you understand the energy of money, prosperity, receiving, and deserving, not just money itself. Money has value because of the value we place upon it! You deserve to receive ... join us and learn how to release the blocks to receiving.

The Empowerment Manual

In her chapter, "The Art of Self Awareness for Manifesting," Melissa provides five areas people become blocked in manifesting desired outcomes. Are you ready to stop responding to life circumstances and begin consciously creating them? Read her chapter in this powerful book and see how you can move past the illusion of the present moment and allow magic to unfold.

The Invisible Thread: True Stories of Synchronicity

In her chapter, "When You Show Up for Yourself, Magic Happens", Melissa describes the magic that can unfold in life through listening to spirit. She speaks of a journey into self-love, the ultimate space where spirit can reach us, from the heart.

Connect with Melissa here:

Art of Abundance FREE:
https://www.facebook.com/groups/artofabundance/

Melissa Corter- Soul Artist:
https://www.facebook.com/melissacortersoulartist/

www.melissacorter.com

CPSIA information can be obtained
at www.ICGtesting.com
Printed in the USA
LVHW031945111219
640174LV00013B/1047/P